Occupation
Self-Employ

ROSEMARY PETTIT

WILDWOOD HOUSE LONDON

First published in Great Britain 1977
Reissued in this updated edition in 1981

Wildwood House Limited
Gloucester Mansions
Cambridge Circus
London WC2H 8HD

British Library Cataloguing in Publication Data

Pettit, Rosemary
Occupation, self-employed.
1. Small business – Great Britain – Case studies
2. Self-employed – Great Britain – Case studies
I. Title
658′ .041 HD2346.G7

ISBN 0-7045-0432-4

Typeset by Scarborough Typesetting Services
and printed and bound in Great Britain by
Biddles Ltd, Guildford and Kings Lynn

CONTENTS

Introduction

The most convincing reason for being self-employed has very little to do with money – though some people dispute otherwise – and much more to do with how one chooses to spend one's life. Being self-employed is being responsible for all aspects of one's working life: to be producer, salesman, accountant and tea-maker all in one. It is having control over both the quality of the product at one end and the marketing of it at the other. From society's point of view the self-employed, whether freelance journalist or small businessman, is a viable and essential alternative to work within the giant industries of state, union and corporate enterprise. The self-employed do not fill up dole queues, nor do they need underpinning by subsidies; they tend to create work rather than otherwise.

To accept self-employment is to accept the development and exercise of a wide range of skills and abilities, abilities which often atrophy within the departmental confines of a large organization. It is also to accept that if you, personally, do not go vigorously to work, then nothing gets done and no money comes in. If the work isn't good enough then bills do not get paid. If judgement and planning are faulty you go out of business. For most self-employed people there is a small margin of error; go beyond that and you could say goodbye to independence. Bristow, that lovable, idle buying clerk, would not survive two minutes if he had to fend for himself.

The self-employed sector of the economy is also bureaucratically untidy – an open-ended, often adaptable area upon which governments naturally expect to levy taxes. More through heavy-handedness than malice they have overloaded the self-employed desk with quantities of brown envelopes. VAT is reputed the villain of the fiscal stage.

Working for yourself is not work for everybody, nor perhaps should it be. Resourcefulness, flexibility and a capacity for hard work are the sort of excellent qualities that are needed (as, ideally, they are in any form of work), plus a willingness to take decisions on many levels. Some types of work are, naturally, more demanding and stretching than others.

Ask anybody why they work for themselves and, more often than not, they look into the middle distance and mumble something like, 'Why not?' It is probably more useful to ask, 'How does it work out?' This is what this book has attempted to discover, individual by individual. It is a book intended for anybody who may be in a position to work for themselves and it sets out to show how one person earns his or her livelihood without, in many cases, much capital, previous expertise or prima donna talents. (Some livelihoods, it has to be said, are potential rather than actual.) It is a story which can be multiplied with infinite variety throughout the country; here is one small slice of the cake. It is a taste rather than a recipe book (look in the bibliography for that), a flavour rather than a minute analysis of the ingredients. It aims attention at the successful (or at any rate the surviving) rather than those who have fallen flat on the ground. It is intended to be encouraging.

I interviewed about sixty self-employed people in the first six months of 1976, following up their careers in 1980. They represent a wide, though not exhaustive, range of occupations. Each one is an individual and approaches his or her work from an individual standpoint; this approach is not easily extrapolated into another, perhaps completely different, situation. Nevertheless, each particular story can be indicative of the occupation as a whole provided that individual variables of ability, inclination and personal and financial resources are taken into account.

A postscript dating from October 1976 is followed by a short summary which sets out the main capital and financial requirements of the business very briefly and as a guideline only. The four groups of income need explaining: A is up to £1,800; B is from £1,800 to £3,000; C is from £3,000; and D is from £5,000 (1980 figures only). Working capital is not included in the summary; this should always be added to the figures given. The summary is followed in this edition by new material, detailing the development of each business in the four years since 1976. Addresses at the back of the book are included for follow-up research.

It is not really for me to say how this book should be used, but I would read the whole of it at some time or other rather than pick and choose. Individuals, reflecting on their own work, often make observations whose implications go well beyond the range of their immediate situation and some occupations previously rejected or ignored may reveal hidden opportunities. Some need particular talents but most are accessible to a fair number of people. This book is by no means the last word on anything but, if used as a spring-board, could encourage you, the prospective self-employer, to take that step.

Groups of Income Referred to in Text		
A	–	up to £1,800
B	–	from £1,800 to £3,000
C	–	from £3,000 to £5,000
D	–	from £5,000 (1980 figures only)

CHAPTER ONE

Plants & Animals

HORTICULTURE

1976: A large garden and a greenhouse = space: space to feed a family on home-grown vegetables or space to grow plants for sale – or both. Clare S, an enthusiastic gardener, started experimenting with her sixteen by eight foot greenhouse the minute it was put up two years ago. 'I grew courgettes in jiffy pots,' she says, 'and the surplus ones I took to an ironmonger's shop. I was to come back the next day and either collect the plants or take away the money. They went in ten minutes.' This was encouraging and she pottered away throughout the summer until, in October, a neighbour joined her and they grew and sold lupins, polyanthus and two thousand wallflowers in boxes. Neither of the partners made much money; in fact they only cleared £10 profit each during the first year, because 'we didn't charge for our time at all', says Clare S. 'We both loved doing it and we virtually gave the plants away to our friends because we didn't like selling them. Everybody said we must charge more; we only charged half the usual price just to get a quick turnover.'

In the spring of 1975 a previous customer, delighted with the wallflowers, asked them to supply her garden for her daughter's wedding. 'It was tremendous for us,' says Clare S. 'We worked about twelve hours a day growing everything she wanted from petunias to lobelia to alyssum to sweet peas. It was through her that people started ringing up and saying "Do you have this, do you have that?".' Once the greenhouse was rid of bedding plants they tried house plants ('hopefully to flower from October onwards'), perennials, herbs and vegetables, which are 'the biggest thing at the moment because they're so expensive in the shops'.

Then a new, green-fingered neighbour came in with them. With three partners the business flourished. 'We've expanded about twenty times,' says Clare S. 'The demand is fantastic and we're now supplying three garden centres.' How did they get into these places? 'I went down with some samples and the chap said, "Fine, what else have you got?" I told him. He ordered things in hundreds. He wanted three hundred parsley plants; he wanted all the herbs.' Friends are still the main customers but Clare S, who does most of the selling, prefers to sell to garden centres and the occasional shop. 'I was terrified of selling the first year,' she says. 'But I now enjoy it because our stuff is just as good as anything they get from the huge places.' The local garage is another customer and has taken three hundred tomato plants this season.

In its third year the business has become more commercial; prices reflect this as well as working methods. Quite early on Clare S found a wholesaler who supplies virtually all their pots, boxes and earth. It is essential to buy from a wholesaler, she says, to cut costs right down. Seeds are another expense. This year plants are germinated from their own seed. Instead of growing all and everything Clare S is beginning to specialize, which she would recommend. 'Don't be as ambitious as we were and try to do so many things at once; we got in such a muddle. Label everything the minute you've done it,' she says, 'otherwise you forget.' A greenhouse is essential; hers cost £300.

The business is not going to make any of them rich. Each partner should clear £200 income by the end of the season. Clare S has estimated that she earns less than agricultural wages working part-time. So how far can they expand? 'Mainly it's a space problem,' she says. 'Even with our three gardens we've run out of space. My first partner is going to minimize the work because she is older and finds it quite a strain. It's not an old person's pastime unless you're retired and simply have nothing else to do. It works very well with children at school and I work while they play in the garden. I always thought that when my youngest was at school I would get a job of some sort, but I never dreamt it would be this. The real satisfaction is doing something which you like, which started as a hobby, and actually making money out of it.'

Four months later: 'We're now supplying four garden centres,' says Clare S, 'and a local shop which has bought all the herbs. Perennials and vegetables are the main thing; there's no money in annuals at all. We don't initiate varieties of plants, we just supply the demand.'

Part-time
Capital: greenhouse cost £300
  paraffin to heat greenhouse in winter cost £25
  quarter acre of garden (between all three partners)
  car essential
Income: A
Formal qualifications: none
Experience: keen gardener

Entertaining in a restaurant
1980: In September 1979 Clare S reached the point where she either had to devote herself to gardening or give it up. 'It was really a labour of love,' she says. 'I was making £700–£800 a year, only pin money for the amount of work I was putting in. My partner was putting pressure on me to give more time to it and I just wasn't able to.'

A few months later, after playing the piano at a friend's lunch party, Clare S was persuaded to ask a local restaurant if she could entertain their customers. 'Of course I thought I wasn't good enough at first. The restaurant had to buy a piano and I used to practise four hours a day. I was ill with nerves the first few times.'

For three hours or more every Friday and Saturday evening (and sometimes Thursdays), Clare S sits down and plays light popular and Victorian music. She knows about five hundred pieces from memory. 'It's a very expensive restaurant,' she says, 'but I get treated well there. I used to play far too loudly, now it's much softer. The restaurant says it's helped them. One Arab even gave me a £20 tip! When I started the family thought it a bit of a joke, but I think they're quite impressed now.'

Part-time
Income: £3.30 an hour

FARMING

i. General

1976: Anthony R lives in the midst of an idyll. The sun pours down on the tender green wheat, lambs gambol in tune with tradition, cows chew, the mill grinds his flour, the loom weaves his wool, and he and his family live off their own butter, cheese, honey and half an acre of dew-sprinkled vegetables. He is a farmer. The other side of the picture is in the middle of a wet and freezing night, bogged down in a clay pudding of soggy potatoes. There are more romantic conceptions about farming or living off the land than about any other occupation. Anthony R receives a regular stream of starry hopefuls, about to buy a cottage and a few acres, seeking his advice. From a lifetime of experience this is what he has to say.

The first thing he stresses is previous experience, 'spending five years working full-time on somebody else's farm. You will see how it is done, year in, year out, learning by somebody else's mistakes. What is interesting about agriculture is that after a year you think you know it all, after two years you realize you know very little, and after five years you know quite a bit and can start on your own with a fair amount of confidence.' Going to college, he says, is no substitute for experience.

Without that experience farming can be a very expensive mistake. In any case it is expensive. Although the quality and price of land vary enormously from one part of the country to another, 'it is very difficult to make a living in general agriculture under fifty acres,' says Anthony R. 'People think they'll buy a smallholding; they say, "I'll sell my house in London and it will buy a small farm in Wales," but it won't capitalize it. The smallest tractor, new, is nearly £2,000 and an absolute necessity.' So how much money would one need? 'Something in the rate of £40,000,' he says, 'absolute minimum to start with, unless one of them is going to keep on a well-paid job.'

There is a considerable difference between farming for a living, though, and self-sufficiency farming. Anthony R explains it this way: 'To keep yourself and your family in food and clothes and shelter you would only need ten to fifteen acres and you could start off with not much more than the capital for the place. From the self-sufficiency angle it is probably better just to go ahead and look over the hedge and see what the man is doing next door and go and help him. It's all hard labour after that, a great joy if you have the mental and physical capacity for it.'

Clearly a farmer has to be strong and healthy, but his attitude of mind is equally important. 'It's the capacity to keep on with something that seems very unproductive at the time,' says Anthony R. 'So many jobs are like the one I had this afternoon which is paring the sheep's feet. It isn't making the sheep grow faster, it isn't helping them to have more lambs, but it is absolutely essential if the sheep are going to live.'

More than anything, it seems, farming is team work, especially family team work. 'Anyone who tries to do any form of agriculture without a competent wife – well, it's impossible,' he declares. 'It isn't so much the work that they do on the farm as the fact that when you come in, tired and hungry and fed-up, there's some food and some shelter and some love waiting for you.' Aside from that there are family expectations to reckon with. 'What makes it difficult for many people,' he says, 'is that they come into farming from a job where they earned £60 or £100 a week and the thought that they're going to live on £10 or £14 for the next so many years doesn't seem possible. They are so busy that they don't have time to spend any money anyway and they just have to live off their farms. A farmer who is not feeding well is a contradiction.'

The cautionary tale below (page 6) shows how easy it is to come unstuck.

Full-time
Capital: £40,000 of which premises might cost £25,000;
machinery £7,500;
stock £7,500
full-time worker (aged twenty and over) £36.50 (January 1976) a week
Income: variable
'In a period of five years, for three years the farm keeps the farmer, for two years the farmer keeps the farm.'
Formal qualifications: none
Experience: five years' practical farming

Subsistence
Capital: £20,000 for house and land
family assistance
Income: in kind
Formal qualifications: none

1980: Anthony R was in the middle of haymaking. 'I've got more sheep and more wheat and that's because I find that more people are baking their own bread. And lots of people want to spin and weave. In fact, I held a class twice a week for two years in spinning and weaving . . . Was I driving the fire-engine before? Well, that's stopped; it was great fun but didn't pay much. Now I drive a milk tanker to London every day, collecting milk from farms in Sussex, Kent and the edge of Hampshire. I go round seven to ten farms until I have a full load, nine thousand litres, take it up to Morden and Sutton and then go back for another load.'

Who looks after the farm? 'Well, I have a full-time man and my son is nearly nineteen.'

A few years ago, Anthony R was frequently consulted by people who wanted to sell up everything and move from the city to live off the land. 'This doesn't happen so much now,' he says. 'At that time it was the tail-end of the hippy era. Now many people have done their sums and realized that they can't hope to bring up a family on a small plot of land. So they do it on the side – grow vegetables, keep hens and goats. But subsistence farming is still the most interesting farming and a great joy if you're with a group of people or a large family. Otherwise it's a bit lonely. Or what is sometimes happening now is subsistence villaging, where one is a mechanic, another a weaver, another a blacksmith – all quite deliberately set up.'

The first step, however, is to get your land. 'The price of land has more than trebled in the last few years; everyone is buying land because there's a depression and land is one thing that holds its value. And not just round here. It's nationwide, because it only takes two or three hours to get to Wales, Cumbria or wherever. Tractors cost three times as much, wages have nearly doubled, rents are £50 an acre. It puts a lot of pressure on farmers. They could be sitting on £200,000 or more. But if they sold, they'd be selling their birth-right.'

Costs have doubled or trebled in the last four or five years.
A small tractor costs £5,000.
Basic wage for a full-time man is £60 a week as well as cottage, milk, firewood, garden for vegetables, etc.

ii. Geese

1976: Nick W has bred geese for the last three years. This year might be his last. Every day he collects buckets of eggs and puts them in the incubator, but every day he has to feed most of them to the pigs. The eggs are infertile and nobody knows why. The vet doesn't know why; nor do the National Farmers Union, the Ministry of Agriculture, the British Waterfowl Association and other goose farmers. Everybody is very interested in the problem: it could be a virus, it could be the food, it could be anything. Meanwhile, instead of ten thousand goslings, which would have given him and his wife a year's income, only three hundred had been born by halfway through the season.

Breeding geese is a notoriously risky business – a high-risk, high-return venture. Growing only one kind of 'crop' is also risky, leaving nothing to cushion you if it should fail. Nick W knew all this when he started but, he says, 'what else can you do in the country with seven acres and £3,000 borrowed capital? You can either build helicopters at Yeovil or sell bras at Somerton or get your patch of land and try to squeeze a living out of it.' So geese it was. He bought a hundred birds from Denmark and in their first year feed prices doubled, but they sorted out the teething problems and all seemed fair for the next year. Then disaster struck: very few fertile eggs. They changed banks, trebled the stock, brought in new ganders and the same thing happened again this year. So, owing £10,000 to the bank, Nick W may have to sell the house and seven acres unless 'men with microscopes' can very quickly find a solution.

In retrospect, what could he have done? 'The same thing,' he says, 'but started sooner. It would have cost a lot less especially if you've hocked your house and land for the privilege of making those mistakes.' Wouldn't it be better to start small? 'No, because the geese were designed to produce a full year's income and it would have done me no good at all to produce a dozen goslings now and again. We had enquiries this year for thirty thousand goslings. There's a tremendous market if you can produce them.' So where does the difficulty lie? 'This is a completely new problem that has never been met in any poultry in this country before,' he says. 'There's a chance that it's not food or a virus but bad management, farming without the background. There are few precedents for this type of farming, whereas the overall principles for running a small mixed farm are firmly laid down. An established farmer, though, would be well aware of the dangers which could make or break him.'

Nick W bought his house and land in the middle of Somerset for

£5,200 five or six years ago. At that time he was working in electrical engineering, but gradually he gave that up and started keeping goats. Goats led to cheese and cheese led to sales in London: Cranks, Ceres, Harrods, Wholefood. The seasonal aspect was a problem: with nothing to sell in the winter, apple picking and working in a local stables helped to augment their income. After a while petrol prices went up, feed prices went up and there was a retail price freeze. Goats faded away and in came geese. There is always another possibility, as Nick W admits: 'The other alternative is to sit on your croft growing lettuces for yourself, but it's virtually impossible, you can't cut yourself off from the world. Anyway, who wants to go back three hundred years? I quite like modern comforts such as the radio and paraffin heater!'

Six months later: The mystery of the ailing geese remains unsolved, though it is thought it could be a disbalance between the calcium-phosphate ratio in the food. Nick W is selling his house and has enough change in his pocket to buy a cottage in the next village. He has enrolled at the local technical college to retake his A levels and has been accepted for a veterinary course next year.

Full-time
Capital: land £5,200
  £3,000 borrowed from bank at beginning, enough for one hundred geese
  geese cost £3 each (1974) and £12 a year to feed
  incubator £1,000
  car essential
Income: C (intended)
Formal qualifications: none

1980: Nick W has moved into technical writing and advertising (see page 46).

BEE-KEEPING

1976: Ken B has kept bees since he left the RAF after the Second World War. He started with one hive and gradually built up to ten hives, then up to sixty hives. At that point, nine years ago, bee-keeping became more than a hobby; he, his wife and youngest daughter moved to a caravan in a Kent orchard with one hundred hives while they built a house and outbuildings. That was a good year for honey: they ended up extracting two tons of honey by hand under the light of a Tilly lamp. Once the honey was in twenty-eight-pound tins they looked around for buyers. But nobody wanted twenty-eight-pound tins. So Audrey B loaded up the car with one-pound jars of honey and took it straight to the shops.

So they have continued, building up the stocks to 250 colonies of bees, building up knowledge and equipment and building a barn when the garage became too small. Now they have quite an establishment and last year, at fifty-one, Ken B retired from the dockyard to devote himself full-time to bees. What is it about bees that attracts him? 'You've never finished learning,' he says. 'No matter how long you've been bee-keeping you don't know all the answers. When I look at a colony of bees it's like being a super-detective, all the signs are there. You've got to go with the bees, never try to work against them. You move a colony from apples to pears but if they want to work bluebells they'll work bluebells. If they want to swarm it's better to take a nucleus off them or change the queen rather than going bullheaded and saying, "You're not going to swarm," because they will.'

Ken B keeps about twenty to twenty-five hives in each apiary which he farms out around the near-by orchards, fields and woodlands. He first takes the bees out to cherry around April 15th and then goes from orchard to orchard as the trees come into blossom. Farmers pay him £7.50 a hive during the fruit-pollination period of a week or two. When they come back from the orchards about half the bees go out on to the fields of beans; then for the rest of the summer they rely mainly on flowers and weeds in the district. The honey yield is dependent on the weather. Cold, wet weather is the worst; a season which warms up slowly and surely is the best. Everything the bees produce can be used – from honey to wax to propolis, a sticky substance used for making antibiotics.

Audrey B helps Ken on his rounds of the hives. 'When we come to an apiary,' he says, 'the wife gets her book out and reads out the history of each hive as we come to it, which helps when I am diagnosing its present condition. She gives the bees a puff of smoke and she writes down my assessment of that hive in her book. Anything I do, like change the queen, or if the hive needs a new roof, all that goes in the book.' Besides essential on-site work, Audrey B is a valuable pair of hands at extracting time. She also helps mend bee equipment, does the accounts, writes letters, bottles the honey, delivers it and collects the money.

With 250 hives increasing to 400 it is a full-time occupation for two people, at least during the summer months. The hours are also irregular. 'Sometimes in the summer we're up at four or five in the morning and then have nothing to do until ten or eleven at night, when the bees go to bed and we can move them.' This 'unsociability' is one reason why bee-keeping is such an individual business. Another reason is that there is no one way of managing bees; several different ways may be more or less successful according to environment and local conditions. Ken B advises: 'You don't start by saying you want to be a bee farmer. You start by having a few bees and building up your knowledge. Then you'll know whether you can make a living from it.'

Six months later: 'I think there's a great future in commercial bee-keeping,' says Ken B, 'but bee-keepers have got to get mechanized.' Mechanized? 'Yes, there are small machines that will help you on your way, will do all the heavy work and the lifting which wears bee-keepers out. You have to see what you want and adapt it to suit yourself. For example, I've just bought a second-hand bottling machine this season.'

For part-time bee-keeper

Capital: one hive, bees, equipment, extractor, clothing about £100 couple of hives could be kept in suburban garden; more hives need more land (see above), transport (landrover or equivalent) and separate extracting and bottling shed

Income: one hive produces fifty to one hundred pounds of honey sold at around 50p wholesale price

Formal qualifications: none

Experience: as a hobby, gradually building up knowledge

1980: 'You're at the mercy of the weather, which is a hard master, and the weather this year, after a good spring, has been diabolical. I was even feeding the bees at the beginning of July, which is quite abnormal.

'We took two tons of honey at the end of May and I hope to take another two, if we're lucky, next Monday. I could sell seven tons a year, that's how much demand there is.'

Ken and Audrey B's bee-keeping business has stabilized around four hundred hives. It's as much as they can look after with part-time help during the school holidays. Even with help and machines to do some of the lifting it is heavy work and no place for dreamers, says Ken B. Many people come and visit them: members of the Bee-keepers' Association, bee-keepers from Finland and Germany, members of gardeners' associations and the WI. They go out to local shows and fairs, taking a stand and selling honey. During the summer Ken and Audrey B have attended the Kent Show, the South of England Show, and fairs at Rochester and Leeds Castle amongst others. 'We don't make much money from it, but what is quite rare for us is that we meet the people who eat our honey – it's good public relations.'

Capital: hive with bees £140
  smoker £11
  veil £6
  hive tool £4
  extractor £120 (the cheapest), otherwise second-hand
  clothes – white zip-up overalls with the pockets sewn up
Income: honey sells at 70p to 75p a pound wholesale; 90p a pound retail at fairs

RIDING STABLES

1976: Tricia G has worked with horses since she left school. Now, with her husband and four children, she is running her own stables in the Forest of Dean. They decided to move six years ago and found a small farmhouse with outbuildings and eighteen acres of land not too far off the beaten track. It took nearly all their money to get it, but hardly had the ink dried on the contract when she was out buying her first ponies. 'It was bewildering at first,' she says, 'because I had never bought horses before, but people were very helpful and took us to markets.' She soon discovered that 'there's luck as well as good judgement in buying horses; with a car a mechanic can tell you if it's right or not, but with a horse there's the temperament as well'.

The school was open as soon as the first two ponies arrived; more ponies followed and business snowballed. 'In retrospect,' she says, 'we were in too much of a hurry, everything cost us the limit. Living in the town you go to a shop and buy something; you don't realize that if you sit and listen to people it's amazing what they come up with.' One of the initial hurdles was getting planning permission and a licence from the council, 'from people who don't know anything about horses. It sounds all right in theory but isn't sensible in practice. I had to have a fire axe which I can't even lift.'

Eighteen horses and eighteen acres is as much as Tricia G can manage. She has one assistant and invaluable part-time help from her husband, who does most of the heavy work with the tractor and repairs the buildings. Half the ponies are regularly giving lessons and rides at weekends throughout the year and trekking six days a week in the summer. There is no lack of demand from children wanting to ride and over the years Tricia G has also established block bookings from local schools and PGL Children's Holidays.

The trekking ponies subsidize the other half of her work: breaking and schooling young or badly trained horses, keeping a couple of hunter liveries and breeding. Like many other people working with horses Tricia G enjoys this best, but like many others she finds that the financial return is small. Even with the working ponies it is not easy to make the stables pay. She now charges £1.50 an hour for riding, which is double the original 75p; on the other hand, the cost of keeping horses has more than doubled. 'At least three or four places have started up round here,' she says, 'and have closed down. I think it's because they've sunk too much money in it and expected too much back from it.' Hay is one of the largest expenses and, of course, the horses must be fed even if they are not paying for their keep at that time. 'If we hadn't got the winter riding', she says, 'to keep us ticking over, we would have to sell everything at the end of each summer. PGL would like us to do more trekking, so we wonder whether it's worthwhile to expand for the summer and close down more in the winter so I can do more schooling and breaking.'

This question of whether to expand or not has come up once before, after the stables had been going for three years. 'At that time,' she says, 'we had a sort out to keep things on the level, but it's difficult to keep a business at a certain size. If you want to make a living you have to cater for the demand to keep the place going. We could do four times as much work but we would be so busy, taking on more and more staff, that we would not get any pleasure out of it. So we're trying to improve the facilities we have rather than expand.'

How much experience do you need before starting a stables?

'Lots,' she says. 'You need to have worked in a stables before. Looking after your own pony at home isn't enough, you need to be able to manage thirty. It's seeing the dangers as well. I'm very safety-conscious, I never believe anybody when they say they can ride; they have to go out on slow, quiet rides. And we never use ponies under five or six for trekking; they have to be absolutely reliable. Another thing about working with lots of horses is that you learn how to cut the vet's bills with preventative medicine. You have to know what you can treat and when you call the vet.'

'Really,' she adds, 'it's all making do, which can be fun.'

Six months later: 'Everything is very much the same,' says Tricia G. '. . . The tack room has been built.'

Full-time
Capital: £12,000 for house and eighteen acres
one pony costs between £50 and £150
hay is £60 to £100 a ton; Tricia G needs eighteen to twenty tons a year
horsebox is useful but not essential; costs £5000
student assistant costs £7 to £10 a week
family assistance
Income: A
Formal qualifications: British Horse Society examinations
Experience: employment in riding stables

1980: Tricia G is giving fewer riding lessons, keeping fewer horses and spending more time on summer trekking with PGL. Her main interest is in showing and breeding and her establishment has been elevated to the position of a registered stud, with a Welsh brood mare and two colts. 'I started going to county shows with the mare and foal last year,' says Tricia G, 'and we had a very good season. This year we're off to Ascot. I hope to phase out the trekking in time and spend more time on breeding and breaking and schooling for other people.'

But, in the meantime, trekking is the main source of income. Tricia G keeps five horses at livery and other ponies are brought in for the summer. Assistance is seasonal: five or six girls, aged fifteen to sixteen, who work for pocket money and an assistant recruited from Manpower Services. 'I've had several assistants that way. I pay them and then claim it back and they get a bit more than the dole money. It's to give them some experience, if they've just left school, a bite of the apple to see whether it's something they want to go on with.'

As Chief Instructor in the Forest of Dean Pony Club, Tricia G is in a position to survey the local riding stables with a judicial eye and her experience and observation has shown her that it is almost impossible for someone with a small riding school to make a living, 'unless they are backed. If anything, it's harder now than before; you would need to be big enough to employ two or three people. There is one place near here that is doing all right, but they are part of a large concern and supported by a farm. Money in my pocket is nil and all profits go into improvement and stock. I couldn't live off it unless we were a training establishment or trekking continuously.'

Full-time
Income: A (around 20p an hour!)

CHAPTER TWO

Paper & Pictures

GRAPHIC DESIGN

1976: On leaving art school Caroline P, a graphic designer and illustrator, wanted to work freelance. She initially gained experience in advertising agencies, one job following another until, about three years ago, she said to herself, 'Right, this is it' – and left work. 'Then, panic, all the contacts I had made fell through, every one of them.' She started from the beginning. 'I had a folio, that's very important, things that have been published or highly finished roughs. I started going round, ringing up every art buyer in all the advertising agencies, just names to me. The trouble is they see hundreds of people every week, but I got a couple of jobs and slowly it picked up. I was on the dole at the time and doing one day's teaching a week, otherwise I wouldn't have been able to survive.'

Caroline P works mainly for agencies; she does both design and illustration, sometimes one-off jobs, sometimes a string of work. It is well-paid work if you can get it. 'You can never sit back and wait for more work to come through,' she says. 'Work places dry up. I may do a couple of months' work and then I'm back to taking my folio round again.' Timing is also important. 'Agencies want work done very quickly; you have to work all night if necessary and it can be very disturbing. Publishing is easier in this respect. I'm designing a play pack which is two weeks' work, but I won't have to give it in for several months.'

Graphic design, like some other freelance work, can be a doleful business without considerable reserves of willpower. 'I work alone,' says Caroline P, 'and you have to learn to understand yourself and discipline yourself and not go under when you feel gloomy. When I haven't got work it's depressing, and I go out and see people and that's tiring and I come back and the phone doesn't ring and I should be sitting down and producing something good for my folio. This still isn't easy for me, but you have to come to terms with it.'

Negotiating money requires steely nerves. 'On a budget they ask you whether you can do the work for this amount. That's either yes or no. The other way is, "How much do you want for this job?" and it's a test to see how much you can get without going too far.'

Caroline P has never had an agent in London, but she does have one in Paris whom she found by a couple of fortuitous phone calls when on holiday there. 'I thought, "That's the last I'll hear of that," but they gave me work a fortnight after I got back.' English illustration, says Caroline, has a good reputation abroad and, since it pays well, it is worth establishing an agent if at all possible.

Agent or not, Caroline P's freelance life has progressed fairly steadily, with the usual ups and downs, although one event nearly unseated her. She was about to go into partnership with a small typographical and window-blind company. At the last minute the other partners changed their minds. 'The moral of that tale', she says, 'is that before going into something new get everything written, signed and sealed before you stop doing what brings in the bread and butter. Carry on as if it's not happening until everything is settled. It isn't just me, I've met other people to whom the same thing happened.'

Robin A and his partner have just gone into business designing posters, sleeves and booklets for the record industry. Robin A is a graphic designer who has taught for several years at St Martins and Norwich art schools; he is doing most of the designing while his partner, an ex-art director, goes out and gets work. It is a balanced partnership, each complementing the other, but to achieve this Robin A had to give up his four days a week teaching. 'I was doing too much teaching and not enough freelance,' he says, 'so my usefulness to students was becoming less and less.' He cut his teaching down to a day and a half and worked at home; now the business is moving into an office where it can provide a complete service, commissioning photographers and illustrators where necessary. 'We are prepared to take the job right through to the end, to take the whole onus of that responsibility away from the client. As a result of doing small and mundane things clients have realized we can carry them off. Now they give us a bigger job and expect to see it completed in an allotted amount of time.'

This capacity for accepting responsibility and working under pressure takes some time to develop. It is not something which the art schools can teach students. 'There's no way the art schools can recreate the demands of the commercial world,' says Robin A. 'We can tell students but they won't really know. The deadlines we impose on students are purely arbitrary. In order to get first-hand experience of what it is like to work outside everyone should get a job for eight months to a year when they leave college, just so they know how different it is. Otherwise it will be difficult to produce a service which is watertight.'

Isn't it a risky commitment starting a business at this time? 'My partner had no option,' he says, 'he had left his job. I am in a safer position, having teaching. Fortunately, the record industry is not affected to the same extent as some other industries by economic gloom. We have put all our eggs into one basket because we have to convince people that we can do whatever they want us to. Once we get that established we can look round for work of a different nature – such as publishing.'

What about working out of London? 'There's not usually so much scope but there are pockets, such as Norwich, where you can set yourself up with a steady supply of work. The kind of work you get depends on the area. Norfolk, for example, is a light industry and agricultural area and that governs the graphics that's required.'

Eight months later: Caroline P is looking for an agent in London. When she finds one she will have more time to 'start various little ventures. I don't really want to say too much in case they don't happen, but one of these will be designing and printing a herb chart – what herbs go with what food – and selling it to shops, and another one will be printing patterns on china.'

Full-time
Capital: none
no separate premises
Income: B
Formal qualifications: from Epsom Art College
Experience: employment in advertising agencies

Nine months later: 'The business is going well,' says Robin A. 'We had a slack period in the summer but it's picked up again now. We've had a problem getting money out of one client. In the end we have had to say that we won't do any more record sleeves for them until they have paid up. We've also been blackmailed into joining the National Graphical Association because they now won't accept pasted-up ads from non-union members.'

Part-time (three and a half days a week)
Capital: sufficient for drawing boards, typewriter, cassette tape-recorder, Polaroid camera and usual office equipment – from £100 to £500 (from shoestring to well-equipped). A good drawing-board costs £200. Robin A and partner are sponsored by another company.
Income: B/C
Formal qualifications: from Dundee Art College and Royal College of Art
Experience: teaching and freelance work

1980: Caroline P went through a stagnant period when she had enough work but didn't feel that she was progressing very much or being paid enough. How did she extricate herself from this situation? 'What I did,' she says, 'was put up my rates. You lose clients who won't pay the new rates and it's a terrifying time – but you find that you get new ones. I now work within a marketing and promotions company on a retainer basis; I still do my own work, but not for publishers, the pay is so bad. If you're not getting paid enough look around, see what the going rate is – and charge accordingly. It's amazing – but you do get paid on how you value yourself.'

Full-time
Income: over £10,000 (doubled in a year)

1980: 'The business was not a success, it was more like an uphill struggle,' says Robin A. 'It was difficult to get money out of clients, the sponsorship deal with the producers of record sleeves never materialized – we had different ideas on how things should be done – and we had to find another studio. We worked a couple of years but we had no pool of money so my partner and I split up, quite amicably. I've been teaching full-time for a year now but, after Easter, I hope to be going back to part-time teaching and freelance work – like before.'

TYPESETTING
1976: Jean W's one-room office is up several flights of stairs in Covent Garden. It is dominated by a large IBM typesetter, planted on a sturdy desk and flanked by rows of golfballs for changing the typeface. IBM typesetting is a comparatively modern process. It shouldered its way into the printing world when offset printing largely replaced letterpress for small, cheap, quick jobs. A typesetter may look like a glorified typewriter, but it is capable of producing type which can be run off into books, magazines, newspapers, anything printed.

Jean W has been working on her own for nearly two years. She started off with little more than £500 and, on her own admission, a pair of very wobbly knees. Her business continued on faith rather than large receipts and it is only in the last three or four months that she has begun to draw a proper salary. She reckons to invoice £20 a day, which has to cover £100 a month rent for the typesetter, £20 a week for rent, gas and electricity, and her initial expenses such as golfballs which set her back £600 in the first year.

Despite the comparatively high outgoings, Jean W works in central London because 'all my work is here, people knocking on my door with a couple of hours' work which I do within one or two days. I know a plate-maker and I do the majority of his work which occupies me about two days a week, all small jobs. Then I do the autumn and spring promotional work for a publisher. The rest is other small jobs. I work quite late sometimes because I know that my business depends on a quick turnover.' There has never been any lack of work. 'You want people to recommend you to others; a good name is worth any amount of advertising. I have only had two spells without work and that only lasted about two hours.' The business takes up most of Jean W's time. 'I'm really surprised at the long hours I work,' she says, 'really for self-esteem and the satisfaction of making a go of it. It's nothing to do with money; my salary is half what I would earn if I had a job.'

It was a big step for Jean W to work for herself after over fifteen years as an employee. On one or two previous occasions she had considered setting up on her own, but hesitated until a friend started a typesetting business and she began taking the overspill. 'That first six months,' she says, 'you're frightened all the time that you're not going to make it and then one morning you wake up and realize that it's a success.' There were any number of things to learn: how much to charge, for instance. 'I decided on £3 an hour and more for complicated work. I've never kept an accurate account of how many hours I work. I'm sure that if I charge £4 an hour for four hours work it's taken me five hours by the time I've done this and that.' Time-keeping can be a bit of a problem. 'I do waste time in that I'll go out and see customers and on the way back wander round the shops. Today I've had an unsuccessful day taking time up with phone calls and I'll have to make it up tomorrow.'

Although Jean W deliberately chooses small jobs, there are other kinds of typesetting work. 'The big, continuous work is more profitable,' she says, 'because you sit down and work for six hours. My friend in the country does books because she has a two-machine unit which eats up texts. Her work is different to mine; her work is large-volume work and her rates are lower because she's out in the suburbs.' There is typesetting work all over the country, but 'the closer you are to a printer the more work you will get. No matter what you do it's got to be printed. You might do work for a large company which prints internally or typeset a society's newsletters or bulletins. If you had a regular source of work you could sit at home on the Isle of Man.'

Jean W learnt typesetting almost as an apprentice to an agency and it is second nature to her now. Is it an easy skill to learn? 'Anybody can type on one of those IBM machines; it's very efficient and IBM have swamped the market. If you buy one they give the operator a three-day course. They tell you which buttons to press but they don't tell you why you do it. It's really experience and interest that takes you out of being an ordinary typist to doing what the printer wants.'

Nine months later: 'I've found myself getting very hard and distrustful,' says Jean W, 'because people are not paying me. I've become very disillusioned with human nature.' Does she get paid in the end? 'I haven't actually had any bad debts, but it sometimes takes months. I now make sure that I charge the right amount, no favours. Perhaps it's as well, I was far too soft and pliable before.'

Full-time
Capital: £500 (£200 own money, £300 borrowed)
largest expense is £115 a month for hire of typesetter (no longer £100)
separate premises
Income: A ('because I've been paying for my capital expenditure this year')
Formal qualifications: none
Experience: fifteen years' typesetting employment

1980: Jean W's business has settled down and prospered. Most of her work is for publishers, such as catalogues and advertising. 'I feel more established,' she says. 'I probably don't work as hard as I did, don't drive myself in the same way. The important thing is to like your customers, it's what makes it worthwhile.' She wouldn't go back to being employed again, but the problem – if you can call it that – is where to go from here. 'I can't really get any bigger; the only way I could do this would be to employ somebody, but I don't want to do this as there are so many restrictions, employment acts, demands for high salaries.'

The next step may be to diversify. Jean W has an idea in mind – to get together with an illustrator, draw buildings in Covent Garden, print them and sell them to shops in the area: 'I'd do it for the interest, not the money.' She is concerned about the future and has built in some protection for both herself and the business. The typesetter is no longer rented – she has bought her own and a second one to act as a standby, currently rented out. 'One of the things about being self-employed', Jean W also points out, 'is that you don't receive a company pension, so you've got to take out insurances of various kinds. I have an accident insurance – so much money paid to me for three months in case I get run over by a bus or break my wrist and can't work.'

Covent Garden is developing fast and Jean W's rent and rates have gone up to £150 a month. But she can also charge more: £10 an hour. 'On paper I earned £2,800 last year, though I don't have a regular income. I just take money out and I always seem to be without any. I regularly invoice £60 a day but it gets eaten up in various ways. I bought a lot of golfballs last year and spent £1,000 on that. You can't solve money, it just mustn't be a problem.'

Full-time
Rent and rates: £150 a month
Income: B (£2,800, 1979/80)

TRANSLATING

1976: Françoise W is French and married to an Englishman. She works from home translating English business, engineering and industrial reports, briefs and transactions into her native language. It is not enough, as she quickly pointed out, to be fluent in another language. She has to know the technical or specialist terms common to any engineering or building business and be able to apply them in any context. The same goes for most business translating. 'You should be employed as a translator,' she recommends, 'before starting freelance, since most translating is business translating. That way you get to know the terminology, what words are used and how they are used. Even now, when I am working freelance, I must read magazines and journals to keep up with current events and current inventions, just to know what is going on.'

Françoise W is registered with a translating agency and most of her work is brought by the postman. It may be a lot of work or nothing at all. Sometimes she gets a preliminary phone call. 'I enjoy it most of the time,' she says, 'but it can get very boring. You don't need to go out and see anybody. You don't know what happens to the work; you do it and send it back. It is almost too easy.'

There are other ways of working. A translator might work in a client's office for two or three days a week, or even occasionally.

Françoise W started work with one company planning to be there for four weeks, and stayed three months. That finished recently – or has it? 'They recruited one translator to go to Algeria and when he goes at the end of the month I might be called up again. I might never go back, I might go back, I just don't know. I have phoned them, they don't know either, it depends on the work load.' And the work load depends on the overseas contacts which British firms are making and the amount of written material which passes backwards and forwards between them. French is probably the most common language needed here, closely followed by German and Spanish. Even Arab contracts are usually in English or French. Fees reflect this. French, being most in demand, pays £7.75 per thousand words as set out by the Institute of Linguists. Other less commonly used languages pay more. Literary translation is costed along similar lines.

It might be unsettling not knowing what the morning's post will bring or whether direct clients will supply work, but the flexibility suits Françoise W, a mother with two young children. 'My children are five and eight,' she says, 'and they still need me. If I don't say, "We will do this or that," they will be watching television all evening. I feel I have a role here, whereas in three or four years' time they will be wanting to be more on their own and they won't need me so much. I might as well take advantage of these years when I am needed at home.' For some mothers, working at home may be the best way of combining care for a family with contributions to the budget. Françoise W does not have to rely on translating but, if she did, 'I would find new clients, direct clients whom I would work for, not all the time, but quite regularly, following up a job, going back to it as I was needed, and learning from it.'

Although most commercial translating is carried out in London and other big cities, there is no intrinsic reason why translators should not live almost anywhere. 'Most of it arrives by post,' she says, 'and if you build up your clients, either direct or through an agency, and if you work at your subject through periodicals, then you can translate in the country. After all, the postman goes everywhere.'

Seven months later: 'I'm still freelance, but for the last six months I've been working full-time for a consulting engineering firm in Epsom. I've still got the agency but I'm not using it at all at the moment now that I'm working permanently. I could walk out tomorrow as I'm freelance, but it seems to be going on.'

Part-time originally, now full-time
Capital: none
  no separate premises
Income: B, now C
Formal qualifications: none – but native language French and fluent in English
Experience: previous business employment

1980: Françoise W works for the same consulting engineering firm as before. She has also managed to stay freelance. 'I was put under pressure to join the company,' she says, 'but I preferred to stay freelance partly because I get paid more and pay less tax but also because I have the freedom – even if I don't use it – to take as many holidays as I want.' With the children away from school or on holiday she needs the flexibility and takes at least six weeks' holiday a year. The company doesn't seem to mind this arrangement – perhaps because they have found her reliable. As to earnings, she makes more than the permanent staff at the end of the year (perhaps because she is taxed less) but is paid less per day than a translator who comes in only occasionally.

Full-time
Income: £43 a day (no pay for holidays or illness of course)

The Institute of Linguists say that major North European languages translated into English would be paid around £20–25 a thousand words (general translation) and £25–30 (specialised/technical), working directly for a client. Working for an agency the translator gets paid less. Uncommon languages, such as African, receive more.

SECRETARIAL

1976: As an actress, Anne P felt that she needed a more secure income, so she took a crash secretarial course and started work as a 'temp'. What immediately struck her was the variety of the work; it was quite a surprise. 'One week I was sitting in a private office with a beautiful carpet, an intercom and the vice-president of a company and the next week I was working for a charitable organization which was so narrow and tight in its outlook that I had to go to the roof or the ladies' loo for a smoke.' Adaptability might be the hallmark of a good temp, she feels. She also feels that secretarial work is very often underrated and undervalued, because 'anybody can learn to do shorthand and typing and that can be the end of the job. A good secretary offers a more complete service, takes an interest in the work.'

One job led to another, at first for her husband and then, after a period of employment, working freelance. The simplest way of getting work is to go to an agency; there is one in every high street. 'My immediate reaction was to go to one of the big chains of agencies, but then I saw an advertisement for a small local agency. It suits me very well because it is geared to the needs of its secretaries as well as its other clients.'

So the agency one picks is important? 'Depending on what you want to do. Medical secretaries are an obvious specialized case. The agency I work for caters for people who are either at home with children (provided that work can be collected and returned) or a mother without a husband to support her – so they put work her way.' Experience helps, but 'I don't think you need to have worked in different fields. If you have kept your eyes open you can apply knowledge you had no idea would ever come in useful. I have wrestled with an income tax form like most people. At the moment I'm working with an accountant and when he talks about "notice of assessment" or "capital gains tax" they're not entirely foreign terms to me.'

At one time there was so much demand for secretaries that agencies sprang up overnight. In more stringent times there is still work, but the boom is over. 'I think that initially you've got to accept what is offered to you and show willing to the agency. In the three months since I started I have been extremely busy, even though November is reckoned to be a bad time. I think if you do good work it is recognized and people ask for you again. There is a subtle balance of letting the agency know you exist by going in once a week and never going near them. You need to keep the freshness of the contact without making them sick to death of you.'

Anne P has another interest, singing, and this is one of the reasons why she left her job and turned freelance. She squeezed a piano into her small flat and gives singing lessons at home. The agency work fits in well with other commitments. 'I have a certain amount of control over my time,' she says. 'The agency recognizes that some people may have careers which aren't self-supporting and they are prepared to give you back-up work.'

There are other ways of finding work besides going through an agency, such as advertising in the local paper, but 'at least working through an agency you're sure of getting paid'. One type of work to avoid is typing envelopes or mailing lists at home. It can pay as little as 85p an hour. The more usual secretarial rate is about £1.30. Although Anne P relies on the agency for work, 'if you're self-employed you do have to set up the business side in a small way. I've thought of getting some cards printed with name, address, telephone number and stating that one offered a fully comprehensive secretarial service. I would keep a pocketful with me constantly and offer them to people – get recommendations that way.'

Ten months later: 'I'm starting a new job tomorrow,' says Anne P. Why did she give up working freelance? 'I felt I didn't have enough commitment to the work outside a full-time job,' she says. 'All the same, working freelance gave me the opportunity of practising other skills, administrative skills, which I shall be using in my new job.'

Full-time
Capital: none; electric typewriter useful
no separate premises
Income: B
Formal qualifications: six-months secretarial course
Experience: previous employment

1980: Anne P is still working in the same job.

EDITORIAL RESEARCH
1976: Like most research, this is detective work: finding pictures and background information for use in books, magazines, documentaries and advertising. Although there are well-known sources of pictures it can mean hunting down photographs in the most unlikely places – a job which is largely hard work with the occasional revelation.

There is no one recognized method of becoming a researcher. Angela M arrived at it in the most haphazard way. She got advice from a fellow researcher and then 'I told everybody I knew that I wanted to be a picture researcher and a couple of people came up with a couple of jobs.' Along the way she acquired a flat full of reference books, a telephone and a typewriter, the tools of her trade.

Angela M has been a researcher for four years. Her first job was researching into 1930s cinemas for a documentary. Did she know anything about 1930s cinemas? 'Not to start with. I just got all the books on cinema, I joined the Cinema Theatre Association, spoke to the Historic Buildings Commission. This was just factual research. I did take some photographs but the idea was to find out about them, where they were, who built them and what they looked like.' If specialized knowledge is not needed then tenacity, resourcefulness and an ability to judge each picture on its merits are vital. A book of eighteenth-century ballads followed from Penguin Education and Angela M was asked to find Victorian and Edwardian photographs to illustrate it. She went all over England, to museums, libraries and collections of photographs. After nine months of working with Penguin, she knew her business. 'Most researchers have been employed before turning freelance but it's not essential and, touch wood, I have never been out of work.' Through another researcher she got a job working on a biography of Kate Greenaway. 'There is another biography written in 1906 and I had to find out if it was accurate. I found out where she lived from street directories, looked at old maps and read letters in the Public Records Office.' The book, however, never crystallized.

About eighteen months ago publishers started cutting their lists, especially expensive books with pictures. This is one of the perennial problems, ensuring a supply of work, since the amount available depends on whether publishers and others are expanding or contracting. 'In some ways, though,' says Angela M, 'it works better for freelancers, since publishers may have got rid of staff and use freelancers for each particular job.' It also helps to be able to turn a hand to anything. In her time as a researcher Angela M has worked for a weekly psychology publication, the *New Scientist* and BBC Publications and has found pictures and written copy for promotional wraparounds for Summer County Margarine ('on birds, animals, butterflies and places to go in the country').

There is little security in it. A job could be finishing one week and there's no knowing whether something will turn up for the next. But the phone goes and 'you go along to see the editor and he gives you a manuscript. At this stage a good picture researcher could save an editor a lot of time and money by advising on such things as reproduction rights and fees. He will either want something specifically or he tells you something like, "I want this many pictures, so many colour, so many black and white," and he might tell you what he doesn't want, like engravings. Then you take the manuscript home and make a picture list and decide what the main subjects and people are. When you have a picture list you get books on the subject. You get an idea of the main sources and, since you know about them, everybody else knows about them, some pictures turn up time and again. Some of them will be there because they're the only pictures available. The editor also tells you what the budget is and if it's small you only have time to get in well-known pictures. Otherwise you hunt around and see what you can dig up.'

The digging up is a large part of a researcher's skill. The basic picture sources can be found in a number of handbooks but there are always new out-of-the-way sources to be discovered. One last question: does a researcher have to live in London? 'I think you probably do, or at least near a big city with advertising or publishing work and near sources of pictures. It is probably not work, except occasionally, for someone in the country.'

Nine months later: 'I've just finished a six-month stint at the BBC,' says Angela M, 'researching pictures for *The Age of Uncertainty*. It's by J. K. Galbraith and it's going to be shown in January. Now I'm doing bits and pieces; there might be a bigger project coming up soon. I think you ought to say there isn't that much work available at the moment unless you're very well organized.'

Full-time
Capital: none
  desk and typewriter essential
  reference books around £50 (useful but not essential)
  no separate premises
Income: B/C
Formal qualifications: none

1980: Up to the end of 1979 Angela M was doing very well, turning down work and employing secretarial assistance. Then she dropped it all to go to Thailand to make a short documentary film, part-sponsored by the BBC, about one of the hill tribes. 'My parents then took me to New Zealand and I did a little work and took lots of photographs which I hope to sell. Since coming back I've run round and told everybody that I'm here and I've been offered dribs and drabs, but nothing very long-term. I was away for five months but, even if I hadn't been away, I think the same thing would have happened – everybody is cutting down on projects. Really, I want to move into film research, though maybe now is not the time.'

Full-time
Income: D ('though that was last year; what it will be this year I don't know')

PHOTOGRAPHY

1976: Professional photographers are the archivists of the visual world. They present portraits or weddings, fashion or interiors, landscapes or photo-journalism for publishers of magazines, books or newspapers, travel agents, industry, architects and individuals. It is both highly technical and surrounded by an aura of art.

Anybody can press a button, but where do the good photographers come from? There is no educational slip-stream to success. Colleges can teach techniques but not that flash of intuition; an assistant to an established photographer could learn more. Others fall in love with their first camera and carry on loving. John M began taking pictures when he was fifteen and then, in his first job with a diamond company, was called in to photograph their products. That decided him; he worked in darkrooms developing other people's work and, in his spare time, branched into colour photography, taking pictures for Candlemakers Supplies. It was very gradual – developing skills, building up experience and slide collections – until a year ago when his job came to an end. He went freelance.

If John M's photographic education was home-grown, then Sam S's was a fluke. After a heart attack at twenty-eight he convalesced over a Box Brownie in a darkroom in the garage, following instructions in books as he went. If he needed to know about colour he got another book. John Makepeace, the furniture designer, was his first regular client. Other work followed, leading to a job with Marks and Spencer to photograph a fashion Dickens centenary year. It was all heart in mouth to begin with, but it won him an award and more work – most of it fashion and interiors.

Sam S is fortunate in that he has another career (see page 49) and another income. For John M, with a wife and child, it was quite a plunge. 'You can't count on anything,' he says. 'I had some capital to start with, but after this year I shall have to pay my way.' Soon after he began on his own, Search Press asked him to photograph crafts for a series of books; he is on the fourth book. Meanwhile, he takes pictures of Norfolk and Cornwall and pictures of children. What can be done with these? 'I send them away to magazines – I've got some in photographic magazines in Australia – or I can send them to an agency. In either case they might sit on them for a year or so and even then not publish them. Really, it all goes back to foot-slogging around with a portfolio, finding out about the market, who to go to. For example, there's not a good stock of pictures of farm animals – not much good for me, I don't live in the country, but that's the sort of thing worth knowing about.'

Marketing pictures can eat up more time than taking them. 'I might be working two days a week,' says John M, 'and then I've got to go backwards and forwards. I'm seeing my publisher today; it will take me an hour there, an hour back and two hours talking. It all takes time.'

It also takes money. John M's work is largely small-scale table-top photography in his own home, but it is an expensive business to finance a studio. Sam S speaks from experience. 'If you have a studio you need at least five hundred square feet including a darkroom. Even if you share a studio with somebody you're talking about a minimum of £20 a week outgoings and £6,000 investment in equipment and transport. Now you either buy equipment and organize yourself, which costs money, or you can be a man with a camera who sets himself up with £100 to £1,000. In that case you're competing with all the amateurs or ex-art students who also have cameras.'

Nine months later: 'I'm working two or three days a week for Candlemakers Supplies,' says John M. 'I have a studio there and I can use it for other work as well.'

Full-time
Capital: camera cost £200
  darkroom equipment cost £50
  use of studio
Income: B

Formal qualifications: none
Experience: previous employment

Eight months later: 'The photography business is continuing quite well,' says Sam S. 'It's hard times for everybody at the moment. The thing to remember for anybody starting up is don't skimp on equipment, keep overheads low and don't borrow money.'

Part-time
Capital: equipment is usually imported so prices have shot up
 35 mill. camera system from £1,100
 enlarger £600 plus lenses from £8 to £200
 electronic flash system from £500 plus heads
 equipment for studio £1,100
 studio fittings £200
 electricity fittings £100
 glazer £100
 drier £40
 studio 450 square feet minimum
 transport essential to carry equipment
Income: C
Formal qualifications: none

1980: In London, Sam S lives in the basement of a six-storey house which he recently bought. There are sitting tenants between his flat and the studio above. He reckons that he has probably made £40,000 profit on the house: 'I look on this as my retirement fund,' he says.

In the meantime, upstairs in the studio, he has developed a photographic technique called front projection. 'You enter into modern art, into the realms of surreal art,' he enthuses, but you also enter into a world where a girl can be seen walking on a Tahitian beach without having left the studio. Bayer Chemicals, for instance, asked him to photograph bodies getting progressively tanned. Sam S says that nobody else has perfected this technique so that, naturally enough, he's got the edge. It is mainly fashion work, some PR but mostly the more lucrative advertising. Manufacturers pay him to promote their equipment.

Despite the retirement fund, Sam S says he has never been so poor in his life, 'and yet I've bought the house and a lot of equipment for the studio. On paper I earn £6,000 a year, but I have two houses and three vehicles. Everything in London – because I work here – has been set off against tax and it's for tax reasons that I keep my income as low as possible.'

There is a lot of aggravation now, he feels, in being self-employed. For a start the Inland Revenue may decide to investigate – as they did with him. 'They do this with one in ten self-employed people. They throw lots of balls at you and you spend months chasing round after the answers. There was a time when there was a return for putting in the hard work. That return is being eroded, not just by taxes but by the economy generally and by the time one has to spend working for the government – VAT. It hasn't got any better and in fact it's probably got worse. As I get older and lose a certain amount of drive, I wonder if it's worth it.'

If he was offered a good job which was well paid and had lots of perks, where he could do more or less what he wanted, would be take it?

'I would be tempted – but also I visualize that in my lifetime people won't go out to work, they'll work from home, lead a different life-style. Of course there's a possibility of becoming more insular that way. But I have a tendency to be a workaholic and I have a feeling that, no matter what business I went into, I would work the same way. I believe that success is through hard work rather than luck, so you keep ploughing away even when you feel that you're not getting anywhere. If you keep chipping away at a wall you know that eventually you're going to get through, providing that the tools don't break down and you get enough food to eat while you chip.'

Part-time (see page 51)
Income: D (£6,000)

COMPUTER PROGRAMMING

1976: Alan F had been up all night in the company of a computer programme. He packs in forty or fifty hours a week working freelance on a computer system for a tobacco importer. Computer science is an absorbing and challenging discipline with its own language and methodology: absorbing for its adherents, mystifying to outsiders. 'There are basically two types of programming,' says Alan F, 'scientific and commercial. The commercial is mainly payrolls and stocks, money and units. A computer can arrange data such as orders and invoices, it can maintain files and provide material for long-term analysis, and it can prepare reports for management. In other words, it can deal with all the needs and requirements of the company. For example, two typists could type out labels to go on orders. The computer could do the orders and as a spin-off print the labels in three or four minutes.' In scientific programming, on the other hand, 'you're dealing with fractional parts. Engineering formulae, for example, may have great strings of variables, amazing calculations; you may need to find the square root of something to a really accurate figure. In commercial programming these things aren't done, you don't need to find the square root of anyone's payroll.'

Many people working with computers are young. 'They've only been out of university a couple of years, everything is new in the business. Someone can work on a project for a year and find something new and it's been staring him in the face all the time.' Alan F did not go to university, he got a job with London University Computing Services in 1972. 'I was lucky, I had done maths and a bit of statistics and computer science and I was put under the guidance of a whiz-kid statistician economist who showed me how systems work. I learnt as I went along.' Could anybody walk into a job like that? 'No, especially now, there's been a recession in big, centralized computers which have become uneconomic except for specific tasks. Work is still available, though. There are lots of ads in papers offering so many thousands after so many months' training. Watch out for some of these ads; they could be agencies with bogus jobs.' It is also city work. 'All the computers are in Bristol, London, Birmingham, Manchester, places like that; there aren't any in the countryside, you don't need a computer to plough a field.'

After two years Alan F had worked on statistics, compiling and graphics and thought he had learnt as much as he needed. He tried one job in Hanover and then another with a small company working on mini computers. It was commercial work on a shoestring budget. When the company could no longer afford to keep him he went freelance. 'It's always something that programmers bear in mind,' he says. 'You may have experience in a particular field which isn't needed by one company full-time, you would be wasted, but they may need you for one month a year. The work is there if you've got experience. You might be employed on a part-time basis, but what they are more likely to want is some months' continuous work from you.'

In the near future, hardware (computers) is going to drop dramatically in price rather like the pocket calculator. This opens up a number of possibilities: one, that hardware manufacturers, finding their profits low on hardware, start selling ready-made software (programmes) thus cutting out the freelance programmer, and two, that cheaper computers will generate experiment and invention and the employment of freelancers. All sorts of things could happen – it's that kind of market – but, nevertheless, the more general your skills the easier it is to get work. Specialized skills and experience with rare machines are more difficult to transfer. 'If you go to a new machine,' says Alan F, 'you can use fifty per cent of what you already know. The rest has to be learnt.'

Freelance work is a mixed blessing for some. 'It has headaches and advantages,' he says. 'Firstly, will you be able to get enough work, sell enough of your time? Secondly, you have to deal with tax, be meticulous about handling books. The advantages are working only when the work is there. I don't like to be in a job where I'm not used.' Besides invoices and time-sheets he keeps a record of useful contacts and conversations about work. Charges are set out at £2.50 an hour, £2 minimum, £3 possible. 'Usually people like to pay out by the hour because it's more important to get everything right than to save a bit on time.'

Seven months later: 'I'm still working freelance for the tobacco importers,' says Alan F. 'The future is hazy but the system I'm working on has become comprehensive and saleable. If it takes off I would be employed by a number of companies, including one with fifty warehouse branches. We've already had demonstrations for interested parties.'

Full-time
Capital: none
  no separate premises
Income: C
Formal qualifications: relevant A levels
Experience: previous employment

1980: Alan F has moved to Tunbridge Wells and is employed in Sevenoaks by the company working on mini computers. 'I became self-employed because the company could not afford to employ me at the time and because freelance work was there. That lasted eighteen months. Then the company started expanding and needed a project leader; it was a big project and I went back there. I've done two more projects since then and the work is increasing rapidly.'

BOOK-KEEPING

1976: Michael K has fingers in several pies, all to do with money, but his bread-and-butter pie is a book-keeping service for other self-employed people and small businesses. It was never intended to be that way. He was originally a banker with London and County Securities, which folded in 1973, leaving Michael K on the street with a living to earn. He tried financial consultancy, which worked quite well until the economic situation worsened, and then turned to company searches (which he still does); now he has added book-keeping to his other activities and in a couple of weeks he starts a computerized payroll.

The book-keeping work is for individuals or small companies, architects, designers, builders and so on, collecting the invoices once a month and writing up the books. Very often VAT demands precipitate a call for help. Michael K advertises for clients and they answer the ads at the rate of about four a month. About a quarter are one-off jobs and the rest continue. 'A lot of people say, "I'm two years behind." So you get them up to date and they say, "Fine, I can see how it's done, it's easy," which it is, so they do it themselves. Others say, "You've got it up to date, fine, keep on coming because we don't want the hassle of knowing about it." I've just come here straight from a new client. He has a neurosis about opening bank statements and income tax forms. There was a bundle of envelopes – about thirty bank statements, four letters from the tax man and the renewal of his wife's motor-car licence. All he wants is for me to go round once a month, open any brown envelopes, say how much he has earned, how much money he owes and who he should pay.' This anxiety about brown envelopes is not that unusual, apparently. 'Some people don't understand money, don't want to know, close their eyes to it,' he says.

Most of Michael K's work is straightforward book-keeping. 'Anybody who can write up books can provide a book-keeping service. You might not produce a set of accounts, but in nine cases out of ten they don't need a set of accounts. Fundamentally, all any small business needs to know on the financial side is how much money does it owe and how much is it owed, because the difference between these is solvency and non-solvency.'

For one firm of architects Michael K does a monthly analysis of hours spent on each project to help the firm invoice clients. He also provides a cash-flow forecast so the firm can go to the bank and say, 'This is how money is going to come in and go out over the next year. We need X number of pounds for these peak periods. On the basis of the cash flow we can repay it within a year.' That is a bit more than book-keeping, isn't it? 'Yes, even small companies sometimes need financial advice but could not employ somebody with my skills and experience; they could, and should, afford to employ somebody on a part-time basis, once a month, or every three months.' Arranging fees, says Michael K, is a matter of 'sticking a finger out of the window and seeing which way the wind is blowing. It varies between £40 and £60 a month according to how much work I think is involved. From some people we get more than it is worth because they would rather pay £50 a month and not know about it. One guy, though, he hasn't got much money and I charge about half of what it is worth. It's swings and roundabouts.'

Michael K works in a loose association with other people providing a range of services from business and financial management to artwork and design. Besides book-keeping he contributes another line of work, a company investigation service. 'If anybody wants to know about a limited company,' he says, 'we do searches and give information.' It costs about £5 and involves half an hour of his time at Companies House. 'We wrote to literally hundreds of solicitors and got three replies. But we get enough business. What we try and provide is a fantastically fast service, a forty-eight hour turn-round. We can get information that day which a normal search agency wouldn't do. We can also get technical information which a run-of-the-mill person from an agency would miss.'

The third leg of Michael K's business is going to be the payroll service. Many companies organize their wages and salaries through computer bureaux but most bureaux, he says, are not interested if you have less than two hundred employees. 'If I can get a dozen small companies together, we're big enough for a bureau. I deal with the computer wholesale and retail it out to my clients.' All sorts of analyses can be done. 'If you are doing a purchase ledger for a factory you might want an analysis of raw materials, services, wages; then you might want all these things broken down by departments. It's like keeping a set of books: you have wages in one column, national insurance in another, electricity, rates, rent and the rest. What I can do is provide that analysis for six different people all at the same time. The computer looks on me as one client with six different departments.'

Seven months later: 'After three and a half years,' says Michael K, 'Customs and Excise expect people to understand VAT and are getting much tougher with those who do (or will) not.' As a consequence his book-keeping business is booming and he is considering whether to employ somebody to help with the work. The computer payroll service is not in operation because he has been so busy, but 'it could be set up tomorrow if somebody wanted it'. He has also started advertising in *The Times* and *Sunday Times*.

Full-time
Capital: for running an office (shared premises)
  pocket calculator only piece of equipment 'apart from pen, pencil, ruler, rubber'
  secretary costs £2,500 to £3,000 in London
Income: C
Formal qualifications: from Associate Institute of Bankers (examinations include book-keeping and accountancy)
Experience: previous employment

1980: 'The company searches side has expanded and we have a new type of service analysing accounts, using a bureau computer.

'The book-keeping leads to a financial consultancy service and vice versa. It includes business management – helping to run businesses. Book-keeping varies in what I charge but, for new companies, it is now a minimum of £100 a month and a business would need to be employing one or two people for it to be worthwhile. It's about a day's work for us. We think it's good value when you consider that somebody earning £5,000 a year would cost his employer about £4 an hour when holidays, insurance and illness are allowed for. Secretaries aren't paid much less than £5,000 and a fully qualified accountant would be paid much more.

'I now have a full-time secretary and another man working here who had previously worked for a chartered accountant. He and I do the accounting and we have two part-time girls who come into the office once a week and write the books up at home, for which they get paid £2 an hour. We have an arrangement with another company doing searches and if you count that then you could say we have another person working with us as well.'

Full-time
Book-keeping: minimum £100 a month for new businesses

MARKET RESEARCH

1976: All over the country market research interviewers are sitting down with 'members of the public', questionnaire in hand, inviting their views about any product from cosmetics to banking, from government policies to children's road safety. Elizabeth K has been an interviewer on and off for several years. A prime qualification for the job is a ready interest in people. 'If you are interested in the people you meet,' she says, 'not only because you want to interview them, they will find it easier to talk to you. Explain what the survey is about, not just to sell X bars of soap but to get a better product, to help themselves in a way.'

This is part-time freelance work which fits in well with other commitments: children at school or husband away on business. Market research is usually carried out by married women with families rather than men or young girls. 'The reason for this is obvious,' says Elizabeth K. 'If a strange man came to the door, especially if it was the door of a little old lady, many women wouldn't answer and they might resent a young woman. It's simple for them if you're not at all frightening.'

The surveys are organized by market research companies employing regional controllers; their job is to co-ordinate local interviewers recruited from advertisements in such newspapers as the *Daily Telegraph* or the *New Standard*. Flexibility is the key note here. After a short period of training, interviewers select available dates from an advance calendar; they are subsequently briefed before a survey, sometimes at a conference, sometimes with written instructions. Then it is up to the interviewer how she organizes her working life. 'A quota of so many people is given, either selected by random sample or from the electoral roll. So you have to interview fifty people, for example, within ten days from June 12th to June 30th. You do it to suit yourself in your own time.'

Appointments are made, sometimes in the evening, and can take anything from a few minutes to an hour depending on the survey and how much the interviewee knows. Sometimes it's not very much. 'You would never put words into their mouths, but you would try to remind them by saying, "Surely you've read about it in the papers or seen it on television or heard somebody talking about it?" ' Skill is required in conducting the interview. 'You have to try and get the person interested,' says Elizabeth K, 'so instead of saying "I don't know," they do know. You also have to judge whether people are telling the entire truth; sometimes they're not.'

It is essential to be an accurate recorder, especially with open-ended questions where every word must be written down as it is spoken. 'One man got very hot under the collar and every other word was a four-letter one. I had to write down every single one, some of them I hadn't heard of. Really, you have to be prepared for anything. A mother might be changing a baby's nappy, the front door bell goes and you're left holding the baby. Sometimes you go in pretty grim houses and slightly tricky situations and then you either call back another day or cope with it as best you can.'

Although working times are flexible this can be concentrated work, driving and talking all day and writing up notes in the evening. An interviewer is very much on her own even though the company organizes and oversees the survey. On cold, wet days it must be a temptation to sit at home in front of the fire and fill in the answers. 'Yes,' says Elizabeth K, 'but you must never fill in the answer to a question, ever. That's one of the cardinal rules. Every now and again the regional controller goes back to a house which you have visited and checks that everything is as it should be. The company relies on you, it has to.' And pay? Normally pay is by the hour or the day plus certain expenses, such as petrol and fares, and should not be less than £1 an hour.

Six months later: Elizabeth K is no longer interviewing 'because it took up too much of my time when my husband came back from sea'; instead she works part-time in a clothes shop.

Part-time
Capital: none
  car essential for rural areas
  no separate premises

Income: A
Formal qualifications: none

1980: The minimum fee for interviewing is £14 a day (to include expenses such as petrol).

TELEPHONE ANSWERING

1976: 'I've been ringing you all week and you're never in.' If you've heard that before, especially if you've lost work because of it, the phone needs answering. The answer might be a disembodied voice on a machine or it could be somebody like Meryl H who runs the Mascot telephone-answering service. Her clients are one-man businesses, freelance actors, musicians, photographers, car-hire firms, doctors, foreign companies, travel agents or anybody else who would like a secretary but can't afford one.

For Meryl H it has been touch and go since she started six years ago and the business is only now beginning to pay its way. 'It's difficult when you start,' she says, 'you need to undercut prices to get work yet you want to offer quality, be different from your competitors.' Many other telephone-answering services just take messages; this one offers a secretarial service, a nightline and an accommodation address and deals with advertising campaigns. 'We run their concern over the telephone, quote prices, take bookings, send out brochures. For instance, we have a client who runs a car-hire company. Over the evening and weekends we are them, we get the car and find the chauffeur.'

Meryl H started the telephone-answering service at home with one client – a friend who ran a discotheque. When her first child started answering the phone, she took on a small office with a flat above. During the day she and her only employee run the office. During the evening and at weekends the three people in the flat above organize it between themselves and Meryl H dashes down if there is an emergency.

It takes a cool head to keep track of sixty clients' problems and requirements. 'It isn't easy', says Meryl H, 'to make sure that everybody remembers that every client is very important. Even the ones who don't pay any extra, we still hold instructions on them; they may be away for a week, they may ask us not to give any messages unless a code number is quoted, little things like that which are a constant headache to get right.' Most answering services run on a card index system, a card for each client and messages in pigeonholes. Meryl H uses cardboard folders. 'In theory that should work,' she says. 'The problem is that people think they know a client so they don't bother to look at the latest instruction – it's human error really.' Are there any clients that she won't take? 'I've just thrown a prostitute off the books – not because I disapprove but (a) her clients ring exclusively at night; (b) if a man answers the phone they ring off; and (c) they treat our girls as though they were call girls. We take up strong references for any dubious clients like people who call themselves night-time security.'

Prospective clients, working out the costs, need a number of calls to justify the service; for some it is two or three a day, for others it could be one a month. In either case it costs £5.50 a month for a simple office-time message service, £8.50 for a twenty-four-hour service to £24 a month for a full telephone-secretary service, but 'we're lucky if we've got many clients paying £24 a month'. On top of that a client has to pay the Post Office to refer calls, rent an answering machine to do the same, or even invest in a car radiophone or pocket pager. It all adds up and a simple answering machine, taking messages, might be more economical. 'Yes,' says Meryl H, 'but not many people on our books could use an answering machine. Imagine that you're in import-export; somebody wants to deliver goods and they get an answering machine. They don't know if you're away for a fortnight or an hour. If they get us we can say, "We're expecting him back in half an hour," so they know they've made contact.'

Keeping the answering service in the public eye is part of the business. Clients come through the grapevine, the Yellow Pages and the occasional article in the press. Meryl H also produces a four-page folder advertising the service. If she had some spare money, 'I would spend it on promotion, letting the right newspapers, such as the *Financial Times*, know about us.' It has been hard work, not recommended to anybody without thorough market research beforehand or combining telephone answering with other work. Meryl H is hoping to find a partner and start an instant-print section as an additional service.

Seven months later: 'It's the telephone bills which are really hitting us,' says Meryl H. 'They've gone up from £200 or £300 two years ago to £2,000 or £3,000, and although we've got five more lines it's about the same number of calls. We had a drastic price rise four months ago from £8.50 to £12.50 for new clients. Old clients we look at individually to see if they can take it. The instant-print is still very small as yet; it's intended for local businesses and our own clients.'

Part-time (sometimes full-time)
Capital: £100 at first (£30 on typewriter)
  £2,000 later spent on equipping office, furnishing flat, telephone installation
  rent of premises (including flat above) £1,250 a year
  total employment bill £5,000 yearly (includes full-time assistant, part-time help and occasional contingency help)
  instant-print machine £1,300 (borrowed from mother)
Income: A
Formal qualifications: none
Experience: as drama teacher ('dealing with all sorts of people and all sorts of problems isn't that far off drama')

1980: Mascot continues to operate from the same premises in Islington, has one full-time employee, the flat upstairs and Meryl H. She earns more, has free time to spend with her children who are seven and nine, and can afford an au pair. She says the business has consolidated rather than expanded.

A telephone-answering service is a sensitive touchstone of the state of the small business world. Since August 1979, says Meryl H, 'the phones have been much quieter than for the last three years. And yet we've got more clients. That reflects the fact that our clients are less busy – right across the board. Last year we needed two people to tackle the calls, now we only need one. Another thing is that, since fifteen per cent VAT, I'm not getting the extra jobs, the cream. Yet every month we're making more money, with more clients.'

Clients, usually one-man businesses, are less concentrated in the arts than formerly: 'More people are getting used to the idea of an answering service. We get more trades people, for instance a man who fits security locks to council houses; he's not the type that I would have expected four years ago.' Meryl H also finds that clients need to be organized. 'There's one chap, a lift manufacturer and repairer. Lifts are breaking down all over the place and we have to tick the engineers off and say, "Why didn't you do that?"'

Her life, she says, is less pressurized. She can take days off, doesn't break her back with advertising campaigns ('which are only profitable if you can employ already existing staff') and earns her money more easily. There's not much stored away in the bank, but there is an overdraft facility to cover contingencies – some of them particularly unwelcome, such as the time an employee stole £3,000 and emptied the account. It was a considerable shock. 'She'd been with me three years and I really wouldn't have thought it. Unless you watch everybody all the time – which I don't do – you're open to abuse. I'm still recovering from that financially.'

It's a precarious living. The late 1970s and early 1980s have taken the skin off more business teeth than any time since the thirties. Mascot has managed to survive, although in 1977 'it was really hard. If I had gone under it would have been for something like another £50. I struggled through, the next February I was desperate, and in April I got an enormous account which not only paid all the bills but my salary for that year too.' It is tempting, at times like that, to undercut competitors, 'but I don't even attempt to do that. I charge somewhere in the middle. The price is fixed at what we need to charge; it's the only way to make any money, otherwise you have to work harder and harder. I've had enough of those days.'

For Meryl H it is not so much the money which is important though her husband – also freelance – relies on her from time to time. Her business started out as a question in her mind: 'What can I do?' The first answer was 'Nothing.' But then she found she was answering the telephone for friends and acquaintances and it seemed natural to make a business out of it. She also wanted to get out of the house some of the time. 'I couldn't bear to be at home all the time but, in that case, you have to make sure that the children are looked after. We've always had somebody living in the house so the children feel less shunted about – I don't know any other way to do it. The alternative is to pay people to do the work so you are just in overall charge – and you don't have to be at the office . . . but I don't make enough money for that and never have.'

Part-time
Charges: twenty-four-hour service is £19 a month for new clients
full secretary service from £29
the instant-print is paying its way but making no profit
Income: D (£5,000)

INDUSTRIAL DESIGN

1976: Industrial design engineering has been Bill M's chosen career since the age of fourteen. Together with four associates he designs mass-produced items, largely in metal or plastics, either consumer goods such as washing machines, phones and toasters or capital equipment such as computers, electronic and optical instruments. The expertise they command is quite formidable and requires many years' training. Some of the problems they encounter, however, and methods of dealing with them, throw light on group consultancy work as a whole.

Most industrial design is carried out within a company, but a significant proportion is consultancy work which brings the advantages of good design to small and middle-size manufacturers. 'A group of five people is a fairly large chunk of pure industrial design,' says Bill M. 'It has to be a very big firm to have a department of designers like ours. That's the benefit of consultancy. You have experience in a wide range of fields, problems are common, techniques can be exchanged; for example, you can borrow a piece of electronics and put it in a consumer product.' The disadvantage of consultancy is obvious: the designer is not on the spot. One way of overcoming this weakness is to arrange an 'in house' service, the designer working in the company for, say, one day a week. 'You have to find out what the company is like,' says Bill M, 'remembering that it is a group of people, not an arbitrary thing. They have certain aims, an attitude which is built up through the company's history, plant which is allowing them to produce things in certain ways. An individual working within the company gets to know all about these difficulties and restraints. Unless you find out about these unique aspects you are liable to do something which is not relevant for them.'

Most people who work for themselves have to cross a couple of hurdles called 'getting paid' and 'getting work'. Getting paid isn't usually a major problem, but it's when you get paid that counts. Three months after the work is finished is not uncommon, and Bill M may have started work two months before that. 'When you're starting on your own,' he says, 'you can't afford to do it full-time, you're almost bound to start part-time. You just need a couple of lucky breaks, which always come, to give you the first impetus. From then on it should be a firm growth.' The temptation is often to expand too fast without a firm base. 'The only rule of thumb is to keep it slow. Get the work first, then provide the facilities, rather than the other way round. It's an obvious commonsense thing.'

Keeping overheads low can mean solvency in a crisis. Bill M and associates were badly hit by the three-day week. 'There are supposed to have been several industrial crises since I started six years ago but none of them affected us at all except that, and that affected us absolutely across the board. We had an overall turnover drop of forty per cent, a lapse for six months. There's an attitude in industry which considers an industrial designer slightly luxurious and firms will always cut their research and development before they cut lots of other things.' Work has picked up considerably since then, some of it abroad. 'The fall of the pound has made us very competitive,' says Bill M. 'We find that going to the continent – France, Denmark, Germany – we can afford to cover travelling costs on quite small jobs. I reckon we could work in the States if we got the clients. Americans are expensive because they organize everything on a three to one basis. If a man sets up on his own he sets up with a businessman and a salesman which makes him three times as expensive. With a business there is a point where it would be financially logical to carry promotional people, but once you do that you stop being able to design.'

Eight months later: 'We are going on in very much the same direction,' says Bill M. 'Our work abroad has expanded considerably and now accounts for about seventy per cent of our turnover. There are now eight of us and we are planning to move into rented premises in the spring – that will bring all the overheads which we don't have at the moment.'

Full-time
Capital: about £300 to £400 per designer for drawing board, desk and draughting machine
no separate premises (top floor of house used as office; part of basement used as workshop)
part-time secretary for twenty hours a week at £2.50 an hour
Income: C
Formal qualifications: from Central School of Art and Design
Experience: teaching, research and industrial experience

1980: Bill M has set up an office in 'Silicon Valley' near Stanford University, California; he and his family, and one of his associates, moved out there in July 1979. He chose 'Silicon Valley', he says, 'because it is full of companies specializing in innovative electronics. One thousand electronics companies work there – its "chips" with everything. We had experience in electronics before we went out there and we've found that American companies favour European-type design, it's in fashion.'

Before moving to California, Bill M made several exploratory trips across the Atlantic. In terms of time and money, he found that there was only three hours and a few pounds difference between the east and west coasts of America. He comes back to this country from time to time as, apart from the design group in 'Silicon Valley', there are two other divisions in the UK: a model-making group and a design group based in Kentish Town. The company structure has also changed to meet expanding work needs. Bill M and associates are now a limited company, with the associates as shareholders.

While Bill M specializes in design for electronics companies in 'Silicon Valley', the London office does much the same variety of work as before. What Bill M has found (and this, no doubt, was one of the reasons for going there) is that the fee he can command in the US is much higher than the UK rate. Nevertheless salaries are '1.7 times as much in the US as in the UK if we employ somebody – as we do an American working part-time'.

Full-time
Income: Bill M's UK rates are £14 an hour; US rates $55 an hour other people working the company charge UK rates of £6 to £14 an hour; US rates $25 to $55 an hour

TECHNICAL WRITING/ADVERTISING

1980: Nick W's geese-breeding venture (see page 6) is over. His A levels were mediocre and he didn't get into college, but he and his wife bought a derelict cottage which they renovated and sold for a handsome profit. With his previous journalistic/editorial/publishing experience, Nick W now edits a small club magazine called *European Kiteflier* and has moved into copy-writing and putting together brochures, leaflets and advertisements for other businesses.

Now living in a house with four acres in a nearby village, they have a vegetable patch, goats, assorted chickens and two Pilgrim geese. They don't make a living from the land and they don't try to. 'Once bitten, twice shy,' says Nick W. 'We went for a high-risk, high-return from a small piece of land. So you stick your neck out and can't be surprised if it gets the chop. I'm not bitter or disillusioned about this, it's just not possible for a reliable standard of living to come out of a small acreage. One needs thirty to forty acres for the kind of living which enables you to have a holiday a year.'

Working in a studio converted from the garage Nick W edits the magazine, 'to which you have to be a little bit dedicated and not too worried about making a fortune'. In the distant past he was an electrical engineer and he is now turning this experience to good use by doing technical writing for small computer systems. 'I offer much the same services as an advertising agency. I use freelancers: writers, photographers, artists – people who have moved out of the city to Somerset. I can pick from four technical artists within fifteen miles. I can grab some of the newcomers, set them up, exploit them in the nicest possible way. I get as much work as I want, there's so much talent here. And my prices are lower than London prices.'

Prices reflect overheads, which are also low. A secretary works one day a week and he has a copying machine and a word processor. Everybody who does work for Nick W is self-employed so that, unlike the one advertising agency in Somerset which has a staff of a dozen, a client doesn't have to pay for 'a slack week or even a slack day, when the wages have to be paid, a girl is paid to bring in the coffee, and all the flashy things that an ad. agency does to impress clients. Smaller clients appreciate not paying for a lot of front.'

Half of Nick W's work is local. The other half is in Reading, London, Norfolk and elsewhere; these are the big companies, 'slow so the work can travel by post though I go and see them if necessary'. Smaller clients include a manufacturer of wooden jigsaw puzzles who had £150 to spend on 1,000 leaflets with a full-colour picture. The profit was minimal but the job was a challenge. Another was a manufacturer of electrical-engineering equipment who wanted a full-page advertisement to go in a buyer's guide. Nick W had to turn out an ad. in four days on a budget of £150, 'which was really very low, but I'm expecting more work from him. It would have cost £400 at the local advertising agency.'

On a larger scale he was asked to edit, illustrate, set, print and bind 1,000 instruction manuals for a computer language. 'It was done for £400. My freelance typesetter sits in a shed at the bottom of his garden and charges £12 an hour for complex typesetting. To have that done in Bristol would cost much more.' So would printers. Within a radius of twenty-five miles Nick W has access to a broad range of printers and one very good high-quality colour printer. Between them they cover everything from throwaway leaflets to magazines and books.

Nick W's own charges vary according to circumstances, he says, but they are around £6 an hour 'unless the customer is very flush. But that figure is almost meaningless. At the end of the job I have to show a reasonable profit. I count up the hours and take all the bills and expenses and double the figure. But it can sometimes work out lower. I always try to get the client to give me a budget and I work within that price. Otherwise, I give him an idea of how much it will cost, but we still usually agree on a budget by the second meeting.'

One disadvantage of the way Nick W works is that he can't undertake campaigns, 'because we're not really an advertising agency. We'll dish out ideas and advice for our smaller customers but for a fully orchestrated radio/TV/newspaper campaign you need a team working on it and that's something I can't do. TV commercials I send to my uncle for a suitable consideration from him – and that means that the work passes through my hands and the person may use me for something else, I haven't turned him down.'

Full-time
Capital: for copying machine and word processor
  secretarial assistance one day a week
  no separate premises (garage)
Income: £6 an hour basic fee
Formal qualifications: in electrical engineering
Experience: journalistic/editorial/publishing

CHAPTER THREE

Shops & Selling

MARKET STALLS

1976: Nobody relishes standing in the freezing rain and wind for hours at a time and getting up before dawn for the privilege of doing so. But if you are tenacious, like Sam S and his wife, market day can provide a good living. They sell lace and trimmings, zips and buttons, cotton and threads at stalls in Banbury, Rugby, Market Harborough, Northampton, Oxford, Stratford-on-Avon and Portobello Road. It started off with £50 worth of peach embroidery.

At the age of twenty Sam S had made and lost a minor fortune with a restaurant and club and was looking for something else to do. His first pitch was in Portobello Road and that day he sold virtually all the peach embroidery. He carried on from there, first as a casual, 'a person who goes on if somebody else doesn't turn up', and then as a regular stallholder. It can take time, however, to get a stall, especially in the fashionable markets. 'In the week I got in fairly easily, but it took about five years to get a pitch on Portobello Road on a Saturday; in the country markets it took two to three years in most of them. In the first two years I was lucky to get on forty per cent of the time.'

Sam S buys his goods from wholesalers and direct from manufacturers. 'I buy a lot job, clearing lines that manufacturers want to get rid of because they're the end of ranges. I used to spend all my time tearing around and buying; nowadays people ring me up. They say "We want £500," I say "I'll give you £350," we argue and I walk away with it for £400. We've had write-ups in local papers because our goods rival any main store in the country. I've recently bought fourteen thousand 1930s flowers which sell for £1.25 in the shops and we sell them for 25p. It's a very competitive business, there's always somebody ready to undercut you.'

Sam's wife, his partner, organizes and runs most of the stalls with the help of casual labour. Her working day starts with loading up the van – a ton and a half of zips, buttons, etc. – driving to market, selling and reloading the van in the evening. She handles stock control, bundles everything except the lace (for ease of self-service) and keeps daily accounts. Sam supervises the stall in London, buys stock, deals with financing and the payment of bills and VAT: 'That's the most frightening thing for small businesses now; you not only have the pleasure of paying and of being an unpaid tax collector, but you have to work three days a quarter for the government just to keep it straight.'

'When I first started,' says Sam S, 'market traders were far less professional than they are now. Today they tend to be solid businesses with turnovers of £20,000 plus or hobbyists on a Saturday who don't really care whether they make any money or not because it's trendy to have a stall.' Small business are disappearing. 'The cost puts people off,' he says. 'Say you've got a stall at Rugby for the morning. It costs you £2 in petrol to get there and back because you're transporting a van for twenty-five miles. It's £2.75 for the stall, so that's £4.75. To make £10 you have to sell £20 if you're on a hundred per cent; if you're on less, which most people are, you would have to sell £25 or £30. I would say that you couldn't run a decent stall on under £1,500 worth of stock. You could do business if you hit lines; if you can buy one thing only and sell it then £150 will buy stock, but it's the clever buyer who does that.'

Gary D is a leather-worker and he and his partner have a stall in Petticoat Lane on Sundays and in Portobello Road on Saturday afternoons. He confirms the difficulty of getting a stall. 'They're all stallholders from way back; their fathers had the stalls. It's very difficult getting a place; you have to have your name down for years before the council will give you any indication.' The other alternative, as Gary D found out, is to be on the spot and take over a stall when the previous occupant leaves. Gary D's belts are sold mainly to tourists and, for him, it was quite an eye-opener. 'I was amazed', he says, 'that tourists come all the year round, not just the summer. I sell almost as well in the winter.' On a good day he and his partner take about £180, half of which is profit. On a bad day it's much less. 'It's a living,' he says, 'but that's all.' Despite the rainy days, the shortage of space, the loading and reloading, it can be a good way of selling and, as Sam S affirms, 'wherever you work it's peak trading day that day'.

Eight months later: 'Yes, much as before,' says Sam S.

Part-time
Capital: started off with £50; turnover now in excess of £20,000
  spends £15,000 a year on stock
  three thousand square feet of storage space
  two vans
  casual labour about 50p an hour (children or OAPs)
Income: C
Formal qualifications: none
(For more information about Sam S, see pages 29–32; about Gary D, see pages 121–24.)

1980: 'The business? It's difficult to know how it has progressed because inflation has been so great. Revenue has gone up but so has the cost of everything. My stock-holding has got greater and on some things I'm making phenomenal profits by keeping them for two or three years. I'm a commodity dealer rather than a seller of manufactured articles which go out of fashion. So inflation has helped in terms of the stock, but replacement costs eat up the money.'

Sam S has consolidated by cutting down the number of stalls that he and his wife run to one in Oxford and Stratford-on-Avon, and two days a week in Banbury and Portobello Road. He continues to man Portobello Road on Saturdays. In the same spirit they have increased profitability by replacing volume outlet – relying on low-priced goods – with an increased value of stock, 'because, as a stall-holder, you're limited to what you can carry and you can increase profitability by stocking other goods which are high priced. It's different lines, bringing in greater revenue.

'There are points beyond which you cannot expand because it requires so much physical effort on the part of one person. The only way we could expand was to manufacture goods ourselves. I make leather belts. I started doing it as a hobby and I decided I might as well make something to sell. Leather belts are now twenty per cent of my turnover. It started off with somebody coming and selling me belts. He handed it over to somebody else who was totally unreliable and I thought, "This can't be too difficult." I went along to a leather dealer and said, "I want to make belts," and he said, "You buy leather, you cut it, you dye it and tool it and make belts." I started making belts. I tool them and I've got into the production of 1930s-style motifs, hand-painting and dyeing – it's much more interesting. Because we make them and sell them we make a double profit.'

Sam S spends part of Sunday and Monday making belts, about twelve or fourteen hours a week, and his wife also makes them. The rest of his time, when he is not managing the market stalls, he spends working with a camera (see page 29).

CLOTHES SHOP

1976: Barbara P's shop is full of flowing dresses, smocks, caftans, bags and wooden beads. Although she had only been open a month, the shop is the outcome of several years' work.

Stocking both her own designs and those of other suppliers, the shop developed out of Barbara P's work at home making custom-made clothes. Demand outgrew her flat, people were ringing up at all times of the day and night, so she decided to find a workshop, somewhere a bit more accessible and public. Instead, she saw an advertisement in *Exchange & Mart* for a shop with flat above, an eighteen-year lease for £4,500.

She bought it. 'It was reasonably cheap,' says Barbara P, 'and although the lease isn't very long you will know whether it is going to work within about three years. I also wanted to live near where I worked, otherwise I just waste time going backwards and forwards.' Having decided to cross the watershed that lies between working freelance and running a business, Barbara P found that events just slotted into place. She already had a quarter of the capital and she borrowed the rest: 'The bank manager decided to take a chance on me.' The man who sold her the lease had started off in business fifteen years earlier and was happy to help with advice. 'There are many people,' she says, 'who, if you ask, "What do you think is the best thing to do?" will actually tell you.'

Barbara P is cushioned against failure by her work as a teacher of textile design, macramé and weaving. She teaches adults fifteen hours a week which gives her enough income to bridge the inevitable gaps. 'It means that everything doesn't hinge on the shop and I have something regular,' she says. 'If you haven't got capital then this is essential.' She has spent very little on fixtures and fittings, partly because she hardly needed any and partly because 'you have to find out what is going to happen before you start spending lots and lots of money on doing the place up.'

Well, what is happening? 'Up to now I've been surviving on passing trade. Since it was just before Christmas it's been better than I hoped. In the New Year there will be a little piece in *Time Out* and a couple of other magazines are interested. Word-of-mouth is probably the best recommendation because in its way it is never-ending.' Barbara P is considering whether to advertise and 'risk having to stay up all night to keep up with it. I've had Yellow Pages trying to convince me that people sit around in the evening looking in the Yellow Pages for unusual dress shops. But you could over-advertise, get a condensed response which tapers out. The thing to aim for is something steady.'

Ever since she left art school Barbara P has made clothes for her friends and gradually she has developed her market; she now knows who she is catering for. 'I learnt how to cope with an order in the right way; it's very easy to be messy about the whole thing. You've got to be positive, offer a choice, take a deposit, give a time limit so people know exactly where they are.' Now that the shop has opened she is making clothes to stock the shop as well as to order. There is a twenty-five per cent markup on other people's work, which is sold sale or return. 'I want the things to be reasonably priced,' she says, 'although in a shop situation I price things more carefully than at home. This is where people part company, because they put the prices right up and get terribly exclusive. I think there's a good demand for well-made things in a middle-price range.'

Nine months later: Barbara P's shop is flourishing in a small but steady way. Her customers, she finds, appreciate an uncomplicated and inexpensive made-to-order service although she now charges extra for fittings. 'If I didn't charge extra I would go out of business in six months,' she says. 'It's the difference between working now and again for friends and making a living.'

Part-time
Capital: £4,500 for lease of shop and flat
  sewing machine cost £250
Income: A/B (from the shop)
Formal qualifications: textiles and fashion at Loughborough Art College for five years

MAIL ORDER

1979: Barbara P finally closed her shop (see above) after three years. 'I was virtually a one-man band, making the clothes, being sales assistant, doing the PR – as well as teaching. It was a seven-day week, too much for one person. What finally decided me was when the rental was raised well beyond my means.'

Moving into a workshop, Barbara P continued to make clothes but sold them by mail order. Then she met her partner, not a craftsman but somebody prepared to finance, advise and do the book-keeping, and together they formed a limited company.

The mail order, they thought, would provide bread-and-butter, leaving Barbara P free to work on her hand-painted and printed one-off clothes. It was trial and error to begin with. They advertised in the national quality papers, in local papers, in the *New Statesman* and the *Daily Mail*. They offered a free brochure; then they offered direct mail – 'send £12.99 for this silk blouse'. They found that direct mail worked best and that the *Observer*, *Sunday Times*, *The Times* and *Guardian* were the most useful newspapers. But rates are not cheap – it could cost between £200 and £300 for a single advertisement of about twelve centimetres, to include a line drawing, so Barbara P did not advertise every week.

In the two or three months up to Christmas Barbara P received orders for one thousands blouses in all, 'the same style because I couldn't cope with doing more than one. It had to be simple and fairly classic, middle market and good quality. You had to have the stock ready so if, in one week, you had orders for one hundred, you could supply them.' Another company cut and made up the blouses to her design.

After Christmas, Barbara P offered a different silk blouse, costing £18.95 – and this also went down well. 'You need something new coming up all the time and you build up your own mailing list so you can offer a new product to people who have already bought. It needs a lot of planning to keep it going, that's the secret – to keep it on an even, regular basis.' After Christmas a packer came in the mornings who also helped with the clerical work. Towards the summer people stopped buying by mail order, leaving Barbara P more time to concentrate on small orders from dress shops and custom-made clothes.

In 1980 she gave up selling by mail order. 'You're competing with the big mail-order companies. You need large stocks and this is difficult for one person to carry. The only way I could do it again would be with something unusual, like hand-printed cotton or silk, or perhaps with children's clothes. I've really gone full circle and come back to custom-made clothes, except that the things I make now are from more luxurious materials, not necessarily evening-wear but for an official function or a rather special occasion.'

Barbara P's costing is worth mentioning because it was very carefully worked out. 'The sample is important. You have to ask yourself questions. Are there lots of little things which are going to take time and put it out of its price range? Your sample, whether for a shop or mail order, has to be *exactly* what you will deliver. With mail order you have to deliver within twenty-eight days or notify your customers. Is your materials' supplier likely to run out? With everyone of these steps, it is important to eliminate as many problems as you can foresee.

'There are lots of different ways of costing. One way is to work on the thirds basis: one third is direct costs and overhead costs (you need to know what overheads are for the year); another third is time spent producing – either paying yourself or someone else; the other third is profit. On top of that is your agent's percentage, if you are using one, and VAT.

'Another way with craftsmen, where the most valuable part of the item is the skill, is to work out the costing on the basis of overhead costs and what you feel you're worth per hour. Then add materials' costs and a percentage – your profit.

'I tried one other way which was to start with a production cost for, say, twenty blouses, and then add on a contribution which was geared to what I felt the market could stand. In the end you have to do several of these costings to arrive at one which is right.'

Barbara P's workshop has proved very good value and is an example of how an enlightened council can help provide workspace for small businesses with benefits all round to the community. Her workshop is one of several in an old warehouse, formerly derelict and due to be demolished, in a residential area. It has three floors and an office with someone to answer the telephone. On the ground floor are car mechanics, engineers and a puppet theatre. The middle floor is a mixture of furniture restorers and makers, potters, carpenters, upholsterers and clothes designers. The top floor accommodates painters, sculptors and printers. Some businesses are well established, others are just beginning; some are one-man, others employ people. Workspaces are variable in size and all enjoy low overheads. The council has extended its short lease to ten years and the workshops are fully occupied, giving employment locally as well as tuition. The enterprise is run as a limited company by guarantee.

Part-time (Barbara P continues to teach)
Capital: the company which Barbara P and partner set up was given a bank loan of £8,000 to £9,000 to start the mail order
Income: mail-order silk blouses cost £12.99 initially; a second design cost £18.95
a simple custom-made dress sells for not less than £30 plus materials ('I shouldn't work for less than £4 to £5 an hour')

BUTCHER'S SHOP

1976: Being a butcher is a dying business. Paul C says so, and he has been in the trade for thirty years. With the price of meat rising, people are eating less of it through both choice and necessity. In one shopping parade he knows there are seven butchers and only enough trade for two – and the overheads are crippling. But even though the trade is not what it was, Paul C and his partner, who is also his brother, are doing rather well with their seven shops. They are shrewd and hard-working and know all the ins and outs of the business through long experience. They might have succeeded in a number of occupations. They succeeded in this one through recognizing opportunities when they came and being in a position to take advantage of them, which is why they are included here.

Paul C learnt butchering in Ireland, first as an apprentice and then in Limerick manufacturing sausages. He went to night school in London, followed by a couple of years in a Canadian supermarket. Back in London he worked in a butcher's shop for eight or ten years, then got a job as a manager despite a warning from his previous employer that 'managers are born not made'. It didn't seem so. Then the lucky break came: about ten years ago the brothers began to rent their shops. They had £2,000 to £3,000, enough to start. The shops did well, they bought the freeholds and business has continued to be good. 'We didn't have a very good accountant at that time. He said, "Spend your money," but we didn't, we hung on to it, paid tax on it. We got a bit of good advice from a bank manager. He said, "If you're in business and you want to expand do it legitimately and pay tax on what you earn. After a couple of years you've got a fair deposit in the bank. If you fiddle tax you just can't borrow £4,000 or £5,000, there will be questions to answer from the Inland Revenue."'

Like most successful partnerships, this one runs on a combination of trust ('I don't look over his shoulder and he doesn't look over mine') and different responsibilities. They each run a shop; Paul C supervises the sausage factory at the back, his brother buys most of the meat. They have about thirty people working for them. 'It takes about five or six years to build up a team of this size, a good team who will look after the public well. They do their best, we don't expect too much of anybody. I think that's important, not to expect too much.' So how should the public be looked after? 'The secret is to be fair to the people you're dealing with,' he explains. 'If you bought a chicken and it was tough and you came to me I would say, "How much was it?" and you say, "£1.50," and I would say, "I'm dreadfully sorry, here is £1.50," that's the only way you can be. A lot of businesses these days people say, "You bought it, it's your hard luck." Or a housewife wants a bit of beef and before you cut it you say, "That's going to come to about £3.25." "Oh God," she says, "I only want to spend £1.50." So she tries something else; you haven't talked her into committing herself, to having made a mistake.'

Many shops depend on regular customers. 'We want to bring our customers back time after time after time,' says Paul C. 'You will be a good customer if I look after you; you may only spend £3 a week, but that's £150 a year. I want you back next week and the week after that because that's how I make my living, not just to give you some rubbish and never see you again. That's the main part of the business, to get a customer back again.' Paul C also sells his sausages to other butchers. 'Most work hard, but the fellow who doesn't try at all, he goes to the betting shop or has a drink, leaves his business to somebody else to run. When everybody round you says, "Surrender," you have to have that little bit of gut in you which says, "Carry on."'

Eight months later: 'We've opened one new shop and there's another one on the way, so we're not doing too badly.'

Full-time
Capital: £2,000 to £3,000 ten years ago (£1,000 buys enough meat per week for a busy shop)
electricity bill is £45 (to include the sausage factory)
small butcher will have overheads of £120 a week before wages
well-trained assistant's wages £60 to £70 in London, less in the country
Income: C
Formal qualifications: apprenticeship
from night school
Experience: previous employment

1980: Paul C and his brother have nine shops and fifty people working for them. The factory has doubled its output. 'Now that we're in the Common Market,' says Paul C, 'we have to adapt. We make sausages, also German sausages including frankfurters, hams, corned beef, salami, liver paté – continental foods, all pre-cooked. We supply delicatessens and about forty other butchers.

'I'm looking forward to the next twenty years. It's not so much the money, it's the challenge that I enjoy, having that bit of edge. I could retire and go to the South of France but I'd be miserable.

'It's harder now for the small man than it used to be. But if he knows his job and is dedicated he is halfway there.'

ILLUSTRATION AGENCY

1976: Not every agency is an illustration agency, very few are, but all agencies look both ways towards clients who provide work and clients who buy it. The agent liaises between clients and enables A to meet B.

Jill M had tried a number of jobs including telephone sales and selling art kits to paraplegics. Then she met Ken, her present partner, who was working in a tiny illustration agency. She started work with him and in a year they had quadrupled their billings. Jill M had found her *métier*, and two years later she and Ken bought out the agency. That was three years ago and now they look after twenty-five illustrators covering a range of work from advertising to book jackets and record sleeves.

What can they do for an illustrator? 'The way it happens', says Jill M, 'is that the artist comes to the agent and says, "Look, this is my work; I would like you to keep me employed." Your job ideally is to keep him employed for the whole year. Of his total earnings we take twenty-five per cent which covers lunches, setting up the job, delivering, picking up, invoicing and collecting money.'

There is no contract between artist and agent, the artist can walk out any time. Many artists choose this arrangement because the agent can often get work which they cannot; the agent is usually better equipped to handle contracts, royalties and so on; the agent saves them time; and the agent can offer advice and suggestions about their work. There is another side to the job, however. 'Someone once asked me, "If you left here what job would you walk into?" and I said "Probation Officer". We've had one attempted suicide, about six divorces, nervous breakdowns of wives; we've had abortions and running off to Egypt with a waiter. We've lost artwork in mid-flight because the plane blew up, we've lost it through Red Star and the post, and we've had bounced cheques. They tend to use this place as a café; come in and you hear all their emotional problems.'

That is one half of the partnership. The other half, Ken, according to Jill M, is 'the straight man. I think you have to have a Morecambe and Wise act in any partnership. He's the one who has four children, he's strictly the business one. I tend to be all fire and brimstone while Ken will just phone up and say, "I'd be grateful for the cheque." I'm the one who is pushing, getting ideas; Ken will sit down and say, "Let's work this out." I'm the kamikaze pilot and he takes my wings off occasionally. He's never done it so I've known about it.'

Jill M does not try to sell work. 'The only way you can do it is to say, "This guy is available, he will cost so much and he will have the job done in this amount of time."' Nevertheless, a major part of her job is to ensure that her clients' work gets shown in as many places as possible. She says that it is a matter of commonsense. 'I go into supermarkets and find out who has what account by phoning up the advertising agencies and saying, "I've got some new artists, do you want to see?" I go into a record shop and see what record companies are using illustration. Or, if you see that a publisher is using illustrators like the ones you have, you ring up and say, "I admire your book jackets, Georgette Heyer or whatever, and I was wondering whether you would like to look at some more stuff," which they do.'

It is a rackety sort of business at times. 'I'm not very happy with my profession,' says Jill M. 'We have lots of bad agents; anybody can say they're an agent, they just need a telephone. But I want to be around until I'm sixty-five. When all the others are dead and buried they'll be saying, "I knew her when she was twenty-five or thirty-five and she was all right and she hasn't changed." That means more to me than any huge salary.'

Security isn't one of Jill M's anxieties. 'We live from day to day in this business,' she says. 'You have to go out and get in X number of thousands every month before you can even cover rates, telephone expenses, VAT and expenses of a secretary. I like it. I would hate to come in nine to five and get my salary securely at the end of the month. I know that what I'm doing is largely because of my own initiative and talents. I'll never be sacked – though I could go bankrupt.'

Nine months later: 'Since June,' says Jill M, 'I've been inundated with students leaving college and asking me to get them work. It's very disillusioning. I'm beginning to sound like my mother: "What they need is a bit of backbone, learn to stand on their own two feet." Most of them can't even draw. Nobody is concerned with old-fashioned things like draughtsmanship any more, the standard is really poor. But what can you do? The colleges don't teach them.'

Full-time
Capital: for usual office expenses and one assistant
Income: C
Formal qualifications: from art school
Experience: previous employment

Children's Book Editing

1980: Three years ago Jill M gave up her agency work and became children's editor for a major publisher. Why did she do it? 'I was becoming a babysitter. Our artists were quite successful which meant that you just picked up the phone. Building them up was the best time for me. To some extent an agent is living off the talents of other people. So everywhere I went I told people I was on the job market and then I met a guy in a pub who was an art director and he said, "Do you fancy working inside publishing?" So I said, "I'll give it a crack."'

Her list of books is frankly commercial and has undergone a few changes since Jill M arrived. She had no university or publishing background and sees herself as 'a whipper-inner, an admin. lady, also coming up with ideas for books'.

Jill M has found major differences between running her own business and working within a large company. When she was working in partnership, 'there was Ken and he was the only person in the office. If one of us wasn't in there would be terrific problems, we would have to carry each other's workload. Here I can sit on my butt for three weeks and attend meetings and not do anything. I cost the company a fortune, but I made my mistakes at the beginning which is when you must make them, if make them you do. There are systems within an organization and, at the age I am, I don't want to kick the system so I say, "I can bend to your systems."

'Professionally, Ken and I respected each other, there was no pecking order. Moving into a larger company one wasn't as protected as in a smaller company where people understood your motives for everything. When you're starting to project your personality to thirty or forty people and there are only two who understand your motives, you end up doing a PR job on yourself. You have to prove yourself, which you don't have to do if you're working for yourself because the proof is the end result, a piece of art or design or whatever.

'Another thing is that I like to know everything that's going on, everything that moves and shifts in this office I want to know about. You keep thinking you can do all the jobs – and I admit that; when you're self-employed you have a finger in every pie. In a large company there are people who do specific jobs and sometimes I would like to get my mitts on it and that's a danger because other people are paid to do the job. I have to convince people that my motives are purely for the imprint.

'The only way I would go back to working for myself is if I got good cash backing, probably a sleeping partner. But I've become slightly lazy. I work hard, but I love the idea of getting into my company car. Also, my husband is thinking of setting up on his own. I've had my turn and now it's his. You do get rather fat-cattish – it's nice to go on business trips. When I was working for myself I was always conscious of the VAT man downstairs, weekly meetings with accountants, right down to the last penny. In this organization it is exactly the same but there are professional people to do it. You're left to be a creative publisher because you don't have to rush out and pay the milk bill. You're much closer to the economic situation in a small company than in a large one.'

BOOK DISTRIBUTION

1976: Tony B is out on the road every day. He distributes books – books which are produced by very small publishers, books which are too large, or too odd to be profitable to mainstream publishers. He fills a gap in publishing between producing a book and getting it to the bookshops, a gap which sometimes becomes a chasm as many publishers well know. Books sometimes take weeks to arrive in a shop or they may never arrive at all.

Tony B is not a large distributor; he is a one-man business, highly mobile, working from an eighteen-hundredweight van in which he tours all over the south, East Anglia and as far north as Liverpool and Manchester. As a book wholesaler he carries forty to fifty titles which he buys from publishers at fifty to sixty per cent discount and sells to bookshops at thirty to thirty-three per cent discount. He grosses £100 a week on average, £75 for expenses such as the hire of the van and petrol and £25 as a living wage. It is not very much for a hard week's work spent driving, visiting ten shops or so a day, showing books, lifting books; it is the driving and the talking which is exhausting day after day. 'It's fifty per cent flair, fifty per cent hard work,' he says. 'Each week I have to sell five hundred quids worth of books to get my £100. If I carried more titles, say sixty, I could go a little slower, sell more books at each place.' With more books he would also need a larger van, and part of Tony's problem is under-capitalization. He was lent £2,000 by a friend but, since he buys books with cash and and sells on credit, he never has any money to spare. 'I offer a cash discount within fifteen days which about half take advantage of,' he says. 'I usually replenish stocks about every four or five weeks, but of course all bookshops don't pay in four or five weeks.'

Four or five weeks is also the time between Tony B's visits to each bookshop. 'It doesn't always work but it's easiest to make it as regular as possible. I've just started a card index file with the names of all the shops, indexed under weeks, so I can see when a shop is due to be revisited.' Apart from the index file, Tony B keeps daily accounts of money coming in and money going out. He is also registered for VAT and, since books are zero-rated, saves about £40 a month. Many self-employed people get in a tangle over accounts; how does he manage? 'I do my accounts every week,' he says, 'and transfer them into a ledger once a month. It takes about three hours a week and perhaps at the end of the year two days. I don't forget things because I write them down as I go along and put them together at the end of the week. Then, as far as I'm concerned, that information in there is correct and all I've got to do is transfer it into something presentable for tax purposes.'

Tony B learnt his accounts when he was working for Unicorn Books; when they moved to Wales, he started distributing. That was two years ago and he only left recently to start on his own. As a distributor, he had to visit all the shops, find his way around ('that's been one of the nicest things, getting to know this island') and keep a check on his stock. Part of his flair is getting on well with all types of booksellers and being able to talk informatively about books. 'I don't go in and say, "Buy this one, it's on television tonight," I just show people the books and let them talk and ask questions. With established customers I can say, "This is a new one, you should take quite a few," or "I don't think you'll do very well with that." Eighty to ninety per cent of the time I know whether they're going to sell a lot or not.'

Bookshops still buy books, says Tony B, whatever the economic climate. He has sold books everywhere: England, Wales, Scotland, but 'although the deprived North is very pleased to see people the distance between places is greater than in the South and you've eaten up most of the profit getting there'. Nevertheless, small-scale distribution can work well, especially with imported books, says Tony B. 'There are lots of American titles which sell extremely well over here, but only a few shops order them from the States. You need enough money to lay out for four or five months before it comes back.'

Eight months later: 'I've started publishing my own books,' says Tony B, 'which is what I wanted to do all along. I've got five books (four are American underground) and two more on the way. I work on them in the evening. Another thing is the Arts Council grant for a van. That means I also distribute Arts Council funded publications. With this bigger van I shall be taking sixty to eighty titles. I'm still undercapitalized, but I might even give myself a wage increase after Christmas.'

Full-time
Capital: £2,000
  van essential
  no separate premises
Income: A
Formal qualifications: none
Experience: previous employment

1980: Tony B now works with a partner from an old factory building, used by small businesses, in north Paddington. They publish their own books and import books and comics for distribution from the United States. They each take home about £50 a week.

A distribution business, run as a separate company, operates from the same premises. Two or three people work there, distributing for Tony B and a number of other publishers.

Income: B (net)

CAR DEALING

1976: As a second-hand car dealer Patrick G buys cheap and sells dear from his small showroom, which accommodates two cars and five more on the forecourt outside. He makes a good living buying from other dealers and either selling back to the trade or retail to private owners. 'As soon as I get a car,' he says, 'I clean it up, put it on the front, put price stickers on it and people see it as they go by. Or I advertise. Once you get established people ring you up.' The car leaves his hands with a three-month 'parts and labour' guarantee – good value, he feels. 'If you buy a car from a private person and it goes wrong you've got no comeback whatsoever, but if you buy one from a dealer you're protected under the Sale of Goods Act.' Buying and selling through the trade is a different matter; there you take the car as you find it. 'It's bread and butter,' he says, 'because I might not retail a car every week. If the retail side is quiet I can usually do a bit of trading.' There are three types of dealer, he says: people working from home with old cars up to £200; traders who buy from £200 to £1,000; dealers who have a showroom and retail, and traders through and through with high turnover and low profit margins. Cars occasionally circulate for months if they are currently unpopular with the buying public.

Patrick G reckons the motor trade works in five-year cycles. 'We're just on the up now; car prices have doubled in just over a year which helps the second-hand car market tremendously. People cannot afford the change so they are looking for a late, low-mileage car, which is why I am specializing in that.'

There's an art to selling cars, so they say; it's more than being a good mechanic and more than knowing which cars are saleable and which are not – though that helps. It is also a question of building up contacts on the buying as well as the selling side. Patrick G learnt the trade over eighteen months as a salesman for Volvo agents. He had no previous selling experience and his mechanical knowledge was founded on tinkering around with old cars to supplement a student grant. Mechanical work, he says, is easy: 'If you can take something to pieces and put it together again you can work on a car, it's as simple as that. Diagnosing a fault can be a bit of a problem, but that's a problem for everyone. Most faults are fairly clear-cut; you might have to be a left-handed dwarf to get at it, but that's another story.' The job as a salesman 'gave me the basis I needed', he says, 'and taught me how to sell. The main objective was to take new and used cars, take cars in part exchange and judge them for yourself. Two things can happen to a part exchange. You either retail it or sell it to a trader and someone else will retail it eventually. A Mercedes agent doesn't want to retail Volvos. We were selling Volvos so we would buy them.'

With contacts in the trade and £1,000 in hand he set up on his own, slowly at first, working as a paid mechanic and buying and selling the occasional car on commission. 'I spent last April to December checking that I was capable of making a living on my own,' he says. 'I was quite prepared to go back and get another job.' It wasn't necessary. Two months ago he bought and equipped a showroom for £2,000. A car dealer could start with £40, he admits, and 'buy an old banger and retail it for anything between £50 and £100 depending how sensibly he bought it. You've still got to live in that time so you're not increasing your capital.' Patrick G's nine-month gestation was spent 'looking around for more trade contacts where I could buy cars regularly, looking for more retail outlets where I had guaranteed sales rather than having to advertise all the time. When you're starting you don't want to tie all your money up in one car, you can't go to work. You want to have a car sold before you buy it.'

There are recognized places to advertise. *Exchange & Mart* is very good, says Patrick G, for cars up to £1,000. Expensive cars are advertised in *Motor*, *Autocar* and the evening papers. Local papers, he has noticed, encourage people who like looking at cars but have no intention of buying one. Dealers sometimes run into problems with the public in other ways. Not everybody wants a string of cars in various stages of repair along their road ('which is why I got a showroom'). Patrick G once solved that problem by offering to service his neighbours' cars at a discount. It had a wonderful effect. Council regulations are strict about such things as mechanical work, respraying and even price stickers. Bookwork is another hazard; everything is done in triplicate and VAT is hungry for any amount of information. At bottom, the real salesmanship, he says, 'is being able to relate to people at their own level. I might have an immaculate car, but someone might not buy it because he didn't like the look of me. When you start off you have to sell the kind of car you look like.'

Seven months later: 'When the car sales are going OK that's fine,' says Patrick G, 'but the rest of the time I sit around twiddling my thumbs. So I'm starting a car-hire business, with a couple of cars, to balance things up a bit. The showroom used to be a car-hire firm and we get lots of enquiries. I've got a partner now and we shall do it between us. We are also starting a car-tuning service, giving a full diagnosis of the engine and getting it to perform properly.'

Full-time
Capital: £1,000
showroom later cost £2,000 for eighteen-month lease (recently renewed for twenty years)

Income: C
Formal qualifications: none
Experience: employment as car salesman

1980: Patrick G's business has not changed very much in the last four years. He sells both to the trade and to private individuals who come to him regularly or see his advertisements in the car journals. The servicing, repair and tuning work is carried out by a self-employed mechanic and the bodywork jobs are done on the same basis. Patrick G says that this is the best way for a small concern to operate, because good mechanics are mostly self-employed and, anyway, it is too expensive to employ someone full-time.

The second-hand car market, like many others however, is depressed. Patrick G has to work harder to sell cars and VAT at fifteen per cent has taken much of the profit out of it. Patrick G's reply is to expand, to buy a service station on a main-road site which would sell petrol as well as service cars and sell them. 'It all depends on how co-operative the bank manager is. A fairly large freehold site around here (north-west London) is £250,000. Well, I couldn't do anything like that; I would have to choose somewhere between here and Buckingham where I live. In that case, I would need more control over the workshop. For a good mechanic you've got to pay good wages but he will earn you good money and on a bigger site you need the profits from the workshop, from the sale of petrol, from the accessory shop. If I get a site with permission for bodywork I'll lease the body shop.'

Isn't it very precarious to be starting anything new now?

'People say, "Why do you want to expand when things are bad?" It might just be the right time to expand. I learnt a lesson from the man I used to work for. In 1974, when times were bad, he bought some new premises, completely redeveloped them and expanded in a big way. Times were quiet and he didn't lose too much business in the six or eight months he took to do it. Everyone said he was mad at the time.

'Of course, you've got to make sure that you can afford to carry on during those hard times. The more cars you can carry the more deals you can do; at the same time, the more overheads you've got. If you borrow money you pay interest and you've got to know what your turnover is and what your profits are going to be – and if they don't cover the interest there is no point in borrowing.

'You have to find a happy medium. To expand you have to borrow and then it's a question of who will lend at the best rate and who wants the least security.'

Postscript: Patrick G found no joy in car rentals. He discovered that the only way to make it profitable is to use new cars which are reliable. He would have needed more than the four or five cars he could afford just to cover for those cars which are returned late or break down, 'otherwise if you have promised a car and it isn't available, the person you are hiring it to is legally entitled to hire from another firm and you have to pay for it. So you have to have a spare car around. On a small amount of capital I don't think you can do it properly. That's how you get a lot of the smaller firms using old cars running into trouble.'

Full-time
Income: D (about £6,000)
Capital: 'I'm surprised at the figure I used to trade on. I've got £20,000 now and it's not enough. You could double the prices of cars at least. Anything with an MOT is £100, there's nothing decent under £1,000, and I deal between £1,500 and £4,500.'

BOOK DEALING

1976: Michael H has been a fanatic bookman, he says, since his first job selling newspapers on a Smith's stand. He progressed to working freelance as a publisher's representative, which he did for fourteen years, and slowly the antiquarian side evolved. He now specializes in buying and selling books on English local history and fishing. 'I spend half my life travelling around the country,' he says. The Provincial Booksellers' Fairs Association organizes twenty-four book fairs a year and this is a substantial part of the business these days. Apart from book fairs I've been in Somerset, Wiltshire, Stratford, most of southern England in the last month.'

Michael H makes his living from knowing that a book priced at £3 can be sold for £6. It is buying in a general market and selling in a specialized one. That kind of knowledge doesn't come easily. It is composed of part experience, part indefinable flair and part hard work building up a market. Michael H buys ten per cent of his books from auctions, but the bulk of his stock comes from other booksellers. He sells about a quarter of his books at fairs. 'Gerald usually brings me up a box of books on my subject and I bring aviation books for Alan. The rest are sold by catalogue.' A dealer's catalogue is his market, a carefully cultivated and prized possession. Michael H prints a catalogue about six times a year which is sent to collectors all over the country and abroad. He adds to his list by advertising in fishing journals.

Michael A has no mailing list and hardly ever goes to auctions or buys from the trade. He runs one of the few second-hand bookshops in south London. 'People can bring the contents of their attics to a shop,' he says, 'whereas they wouldn't go to a private address. About half my books are sold in the shop, the rest at book fairs.' Most of the books sold are nineteenth century; earlier books are rare and expensive. Some books always sell better than others: those with fine bindings or illustrations sell, theology does not sell (been written about too often), fiction does not sell unless it is of intrinsic value. Books which always sell, says Michael A, are those about old customs or country life or something discovered, like 'the sex life of the crab' or 'diseases of craftsmen'. Michael A details the progress of an antiquarian book: 'It starts with people producing them from dustbins, bric-à-brac shops and second-hand shops. They gradually move into the hands of the specialist. They may go into auctions and be bought by dealers here or abroad, they may come to fairs. They move on. They may go into the hands of dealers again or into universities or institutions where they are used as reference books. If they go to a collector and he dies, while his body is still warm his wife sells the books and they come into the open market again.'

One practice which is spoken of as if it is a secret vice is that of breaking up books to get at the prints. 'The illustrations are sometimes cut out,' says Michael A, 'then colour washed and framed to make prints. It is deplorable for a good book, but it does pay the rent. This is a trade which is connected with investment and the prints as fine art may themselves be an investment.'

Stephen C used to be an acquisitive collector; now he not only collects, but also buys and sells modern first editions of creative writing and books on bygone aspects of English life such as canals, windmills and folk lore. He also has a shop – 'with all its overheads, it's an expensive luxury'. Postage is another large expense. 'We send one thousand catalogues and each catalogue is 12½p second-class postage. You have your American library buyer and, say, he gets six catalogues that morning and five of them are seamail, six weeks old. I bet they go straight into the bin. If you send that catalogue airmail it will cost 50p and he still might not order.'

Stephen C's customers are mainly private collectors. 'The golden age of the American institutional budgets is dead and gone,' he says, 'but I'm finding that private people are buying books however little money they have. There's something about a first edition; you must have it, particularly if you are forming an author collection.' He pulls down one book after another. 'This is John Fowles's first book; this is the first book that Rex Whistler illustrated. One of the great things in modern first editions is literary associations: *The Forest Giant* by Adrien Le Corbeau published by Jonathan Cape in 1924 and translated by J. H. Ross, which is a pseudonym for Lawrence of Arabia, one of his four pseudonyms. You wouldn't know that, a lot of booksellers wouldn't know that, and would price it five bob. You see, it's £12.'

Ten months later: Despite an earlier attempt to open a bookshop, which never paid off, Michael H has tried again. This time 'it's an art gallery and second-hand and antiquarian bookshop combined', he says. 'We sell English topographical books and nineteenth-century topographical watercolours. I have a manageress and it's been going about two months, rather well in fact, we can afford to eat nearly every day now.'

'The book fairs are doing very well,' says Michael A. 'We now have a provincial one every month. I think they are getting more popular as bookshops tend to die out. I've still got the shop of course. With the aid of alcohol and a reliable staff we're carrying on.'

'It's a difficult financial period,' says Stephen C, 'but people are still buying books. We've just sent out a catalogue and half of the books listed in it have been sold in the first week.'

MICHAEL H
Full-time
Capital: anything, he says, between £100 and £20,000
car essential

Income: C
Formal qualifications: none
Experience: previous employment

MICHAEL A

1980: 'I no longer have a bookshop – I have a book*room* in Chichester and it's all mail order: naval, maritime, sea and shipping. I stock fewer books but they have the same commercial value as before. With a shop I was tied to it. Now I spend most of my time at book fairs or buying books and this place looks after itself with an answerphone and a plastic memo-form on the door. You could come and see me but you would have to make an appointment otherwise I might be on the beach, walking the downs or out buying books.

'So far as the local authorities are concerned, this is an "office" and is not a place for retail selling. It serves the serious collector and the trade and enables me to concentrate on books in depth, since I don't have to carry general stock. I sell all over the world and usually buy in this country. It pleases me to find a book in an out-of-the-way place like Wapping and sell it to a Japanese museum.

'The Provincial Booksellers' Fairs Association is more regionalized now, with more fairs and more members. Once a month, fifty booksellers meet in London and there are about fifty other fairs held in the regions throughout the year. Some might be second-echelon fairs held in a church hall – or book jumbles. It's extraordinary how people buy from jumble sales. We sell more there than in our own shops, it's like Tescos.

'My selling maritime books in Chichester has got nothing to do with the place. I'd be more likely to sell alcohol to the people who have boats around here!'

FURNITURE SHOP

1980: Sue M worked at home stripping and renovating old furniture (see page 96), but in April 1977 Bruce M, an architect, finding that business was slow and that his wife was making more money than he was, gave up his partnership and went into business with Sue. He helped with the furniture and then took a stall in Hampstead market selling prints and another in Portobello Road selling maps and prints. Gradually, he became less involved with the furniture and concentrated on maps, prints and books.

With both of them at home with the baby, 'it was getting a bit cramped to say the least; we would sit down to a meal with tins of polish and sandpaper on the table. The phone kept ringing and we were sometimes very busy with no room to display the stuff. The upholsterers didn't like it because I was making more money than they were so we got the elbow up at their market. We had a funny year that first year. If two of you with four kids to feed and the mortgage to pay can keep yourselves it says quite a lot. With the prints there's not much profit in it; you've got to clean a dozen, flatten a dozen, colour a dozen and the markup may only be a couple of quid. Some weeks we would have a blitz on colouring, then the next week a blitz on doing the furniture. The precariousness of our situation only hit me after three months when somebody said, "What are you going to pay the mortgage with?" Something always turned up, a quick removal job with the van – well, it's a tenner in your pocket.'

After the upholsterers' market folded Sue M started selling a few choice items in a craft shop – a side-table, a blanket-box – displayed with photographs and a pile of cards. 'I got quite a lot of business that way. The people who came were interested from the start. If somebody can ring up to see whether you're in on a Tuesday morning you're sixty per cent of the way to selling them something.' But she still needed a larger display space, so Sue and Bruce M spent six rather depressing months looking for a shop. 'We had no capital and everything that we were interested in required a premium, even tatty places in Willesden wanted £2,000 – and you're never going to see that money again. There was one shop that was £40 a week but the rates were the same again. Eventually, we found a shop in a street in Harrow full of other small shops. It was only a short lease but we took it at £15 a week rent. I rented out the top part and Bruce spent four days plastering. We put a partition about two-thirds of the way down to make a work area and the electrician came to put lights in. The signwriter was another £70. Altogether we spent about £500. At the last minute we wheeled the furniture in.'

The shop opened in October 1978. That first Saturday Sue M took £300 and 'belted up the market Sunday morning with the money burning a hole in my pocket'. The shop is open on Tuesdays, Thursdays, Fridays and Saturdays. 'Saturday is a good day for selling, but for the rest of the week I go down there to do some work and if any customers come in it's a bonus. I do all the sanding and polishing.'

The furniture is stripped elsewhere unless it is covered with only a thin coat of varnish or is needed in a hurry. Sue M sells much the same pieces as before: dressing-tables, chests of drawers, wardrobes, tables and chairs. She also sells linen presses, which are popular in an area where many of the houses have large halls and bay windows. She can sell, she says, because nobody for miles around is doing the same thing as her.

Apart from the furniture – mostly pine – cast-iron fireplaces are becoming popular as well as linen which she buys in bundles. 'What you need is something that turns itself over without you having to work on it. Then you want some better-class items, some more expensive pieces. Because you have your bread and butter you can afford to have something costing £150 and it doesn't matter if it takes a couple of months to shift it. Then a few things, like the sewing-machine, which are just interesting, and a few cheaper things – there are quite a lot of people who wander round with a fiver in their pocket. I've sold a few cookery books which have gone quite well. You can double your money on them. The breadboards – you only make a couple of quid but they go well with everything else and they don't need any work.'

The children are at school two streets away from the shop so, if nobody is at home, Sue M can collect them and bring them back to the shop for an hour or so. About 5.30pm she packs up and then often does deliveries in the evening. It is a lot to co-ordinate. For a few months she employed a boy to help in the shop. 'I needed to get out and about more. It was OK when he started, he didn't have any ideas about skiving, but after a while you just don't have the same interest if it's not your business. There was a girl who wanted to work here but there's a lot of lifting, which is why I wanted a boy because it's nice to be able to say, "Go and unload the van."'

Most of the furniture comes from a dealer in house clearance and is sold to individuals. 'I get two kinds of customer apart from the time-wasters. There are those like the lady who came in and said she wasn't paying £15 for what was "after all only a second-hand chair". And then there are those who think that £65 for a chest of drawers must be the bargain of the week. The majority of customers are converted to the value of old furniture, but sometimes you have to point out that it's been around for a hundred years and will still be there in another fifty. I get quite a lot of mums who look and then send their daughters in. Old ladies think everything is rather nice and I try to have something interesting in the window for them, like a cast-iron sewing-machine or a butter churn.'

Along with thirty others in the street, the shop is due to be demolished. Sue M has been looking round for another but, as before, it isn't easy and she needs to be near the children's school. 'When the shop closes I'll probably work from home again and then go over to France and have a nose round. I know people who take furniture to France, Holland and Germany and I have a friend who takes pianos to Italy. The way to export, so I've been told, is to fill your van, packing it carefully, and go down to Dover. All along the quay are forwarding agents. You trot into one, pay him £15 and he fills in a form and it says your name and where you're dispatching to. The agent then gives you a list of what you've got. I feel now that I'm ready to do it.'

Full-time
Income: 'I don't honestly know. Some weeks I take £1,000, then for a couple of week I don't take anything. I wander round with £300 to £400 in my pocket and at the end of the week I've got nothing. I paid the stripper £100 on Wednesday and £60 on Friday and I spent £200 at the Sunday market.'
Shop: £15 rent for a short lease; £500 to make good
van essential
Sue M has a butcher's bike

IMPORTING/EXPORTING

1976: 'The real skill in selling', says Antonio B, an agent and importer of onyx and alabaster lamps from Spain to England, 'is finding out what the client wants and transmitting this to the Spanish manufacturer. Many people come over here with goods, just on the off-chance, and I can see that they are not going to sell.' The first thing, then, is to find out what people want and it can be done 'if the client trusts you. If he trusts you, you will have access to all sorts of information.' The technical business of importing or exporting is comparatively straightforward after that.

Antonio B has lived in Britain for eight years. For the first six years he worked for a translation agency and as an interpreter for visiting Spanish businessmen. He then interpreted for a manufacturer of onyx lamps. 'He had come over here without any knowledge of the market and we started from scratch, looking at directories, trying to find manufacturers of lamps and making appointments.' After ten days Antonio B was offered the job of representative and without any previous experience he agreed to sell lamps on commission. When the lamps arrived from Spain, however, there were a couple of bad sales and to avoid returning the goods Antonio B bought and stored four hundred lamps in his flat. He had to sell them, but there were a lot of identical lamps on the market. 'I decided to change the shapes of the lamps,' he says, 'and I started importing different fittings. I experimented on shapes just to find out tastes, what people liked. In the end I sold them all just by finding the right shape.' But tastes change. Antontio B had a lot of brown onyx lamps, 'which was a colour nobody wanted to know about because everybody had the idea that onyx ought to be green. It was only because I was stuck with stocks that I had to persevere with the brown onyx. Now, after two years, brown is a top colour. There are other factors, of course; green is sometimes difficult to get and more expensive.'

Meanwhile, manufacturers who were buying onyx were also buying alabaster, not only lamps but ashtrays, boxes, eggs, jars and figures. Antonio B found a supplier of alabaster and broadened his range. He added small wooden carts to his list and these carts showed how vulnerable the gift market is to undercutting. 'For two years there was an incredible sale of these carts,' he says, 'and since then it has been copied in plastic and the prices have immediately dropped.' Other items, particularly if they can't be imitated, may have a steadier sale, for example 'brown onyx which doesn't seem to come from many other places. In alabaster, prices are lower than the competitor, which is Italy. In Spain we don't have the knowhow of finishing or colouring alabaster, but in white there is no problem.' When dealing with new products Antonio B imports only a small quantity – about £1,000 worth – to assess the market with an immediate supply of samples and stocks. Spanish firms give him three or four months' credit, simply because they trust him; it is easier, he reckons, to get £10,000 credit from a Spanish manufacturer than £500 from a British bank.

As an agent Antonio B's commission ranges from five to ten per cent. Not only does he have to find buyers, but he also has to see that 'the buyer and seller are on good terms. If the buyer says, "I haven't got the right quantity," or "This is bad quality," or "We have so many breakages," I have to keep the peace.'

Antonio B would like to leave the importing side and concentrate on selling, on 'becoming a buying agent for half a dozen importers because the real importers buy in large quantities provided the prices are right. It allows you to travel and find manufacturers who are willing and able to sell over here and to try to connect the two things together. The task is to persuade the Spanish manufacturer to produce what England would like to consume.'

Four months later: 'I am gradually becoming a direct importer of goods,' says Antonio B. 'This is partly because it is very difficult to return merchandise once it has been imported and sometimes the previous importer won't accept it because of economic difficulties or disputes over quality. So I sell it here. The other reason is that I get very good credit from Spanish manufacturers. There are now three of us. Two of us are partners and the third is a sales agent.'

Full-time
Capital: for typewriter and usual office expenses
office rent £60 a month
warehouse space (large enough for two large container loads) £40 a month including handling charges (handling and storage charges are two per cent of the price of goods)
car essential
Income: B
Formal qualifications: none (in this case fluent Spanish is very useful)

1980: 'The only goods which have been continuous since I started are the onyx and alabaster. When they stabilized I got a partner and he now handles the whole of the lighting operation with a couple of salesmen who work on commission. At that point I wanted to do something different, to act as an agent, handling and controlling everything from my desk. But I got landed with the goods I was trying to sell. Negotiating a transaction from Spain or wherever to England on a commission basis is virtually impossible. These wooden carts, for example, were slow to move and could only be sold once they were here. They go together with pottery Shire horses and I've been selling them in considerable quantities for at least the last five years.'

Out of the cash flow generated by the horse-and-cart business Antonio B bought the small pottery, which manufactured the horses, for £9,000. It was a two-kiln family-run business and Antonio B hoped that the six people who worked there would produce five hundred Shires a week at fifty per cent gross profit. 'But through lack of management and lack of productivity they didn't. There were material difficulties, kiln failures and absenteeism and it was just not profitable. After one year I sold it, recovered the investment and part of the losses, but I didn't make a profit. I was happy to get rid of this pottery because it was obviously not my business to become a manufacturer!'

Keeping a contract with the pottery for the supply of Shires, and with the onyx and alabaster side of the business running on its own accord, Antonio B looked around for another market. He turned to shoes. A couple of years before, Antonio B and his partner had formed themselves into a limited company, one of their Spanish manufacturers becoming a shareholder. Through him, they imported men's shoes and tried to sell them to wholesalers. 'But it became obvious that goods from Spain were becoming less and less competitive and goods from England becoming more competitive. The British pound may seem strong but the peseta is also strong. Every time I buy goods from Spain it costs me more. Sometimes the goods here are four times as expensive in Spain. So I started exporting goods.'

Antonio B found that most of his contacts in Spain were selling goods which could be supplied more cheaply from the UK. They were small companies, manufacturers as well as retailers, that could not buy large quantities of any one item. 'But they can buy smaller quantities of a hundred different articles. So I buy for them – from cash-and-carrys which sell at the same price as manufacturers. It could be crockery, china, silver-plated goblets and trays from India, glasses, fruit bowls, crystal – to make up a lorryload. I organize it completely. I am the buyer for them and I get my percentage. We've also started with Persian and Pakistani carpets. In London there are huge warehouses full of carpets and the Indian importers compete amongst themselves, so prices are low. Imagine a small Spanish trader trying to go to Pakistan and import £3,000 worth of rugs! The cash-and-carrys are advertised in *Market Trader* and other magazines and are taking over the old wholesaler. They don't mind whether you buy a large or a small quantity, it's all the same price. It's very practical from my point of view.

'It's cheaper to buy in England, particularly with goods from the ex-colonies. Perhaps sixty per cent of the goods I export are not made here, but it still comes out at a competitive price.'

For the immediate future Antonio B is letting the gifts – carts and horses – drop: 'It's a temperamental market and I intend to leave it because it requires a lot of effort to keep going – and concentrate on exports.' The shoe business may develop, with Antonio B as the distributor and the Spanish manufacturer holding the goods in his own UK warehouse. 'I respond to demand rather than seeking anything. I got into this with the intention of being a salesman, then I became an importer (because I found the goods in my flat), then I needed somewhere to put them and we got a large warehouse, then we needed an office and then some help. We're expanding constantly, turnover has gone up from £11,000 in the first year to over £350,000 but I have no capital and it's tight economically, having to sell the goods within three months. It's a lot of risk, particularly nowadays when things are slower. But it's quite possible that I'll set up another company in Spain.'

Full-time
Income: D (£8,000)

BOARD GAMES

1980: Stephen J's snack bar has been left behind (see page 143) and the games business has taken off. It always looked as though it might. Starting as a hobby, Stephen J and his two flatmates began making games out of wood and importing them from the United States – board games, table-top games, games with miniatures. 'At that time there was nobody else interested in importing. We wrote to all the companies in the States and said, "We're the biggest over here, let's have an exclusive deal where you don't supply anybody else . . ." And they all said OK – because they hadn't heard from anybody else.'

From that auspicious beginning they moved on to bigger things. Now they needed an office. 'It had become a definite commitment. An office is a regular outgoing and we had to think about insurance bills, telephone bills. We found a little office, fifteen foot by ten foot, in Shepherds Bush.'

One person dropped out as he was more interested in his career as a civil engineer – and then there were two. This can be a strained situation, the success of the business depending on how well the partners work together. In Stephen J's case he has known his partner since schooldays and they complement each other. 'He's a good salesman and has a good company image. I like rushing around getting things organized. We use the company name as a trading name but officially it's a partnership. When the business is small the mistakes you make aren't all that big; as the business grows you are talking about orders worth thousands of pounds. We both started off with an interest in games – and we're still on speaking terms.'

The business developed and the partners moved from their tiny office to another off Chiswick High Road, with a shop beneath. They also took on a warehouse and employees: four people at the warehouse, packing and dealing with trade customers and mail order; a production manager, two people in the shop, a paste-up person, and Stephen J's sister who does the accounts on a spare-time basis.

They buy most of their games from the States. In the early days that meant parcel post, up to ten or twelve packets a day. The post, says Stephen J, is 'terrible, things get held up by customs, they take ten weeks or get damaged'. A supplier, tired of damage claims, complained and that precipitated the next move which was to send the games by air-freight. 'We used to phone through an order and get the stuff a week later. I would recommend using an agent, we have a good one. The goods arrive at the airport, the agent collects and gives us a ring, saying, "When do you want it delivered?" It's quite expensive that way. Sea-freight takes four to six weeks and is much less expensive.'

The partnership imports on open account and sells abroad on COD. They use Export Credit Guarantee, the government scheme which guarantees payment. Naturally enough, games published in the States are more expensive to buy here. 'We get pretty good discounts from the States. The freight plus agent's fees plus duty amount to another third on top of our buying cost. We have to give retailers anything up to 52½ per cent, but on the American stuff we give 42½ per cent discount on maximum quantities.' It works out that a game which could be bought for $10 in the States will cost £7.50 in the UK.

The games are sold downstairs in their own shop; they are also sold by mail order to individuals and distributed to other shops.

'When we started off, it must have been eighty per cent mail order, twenty per cent distribution. Now it's the other way round. There are only about three or four companies in the field and most of them have concentrated either on mail order or distribution. With mail order you get to the point where you're reaching everybody through magazines and your own mail shots, but there's a certain number of people who won't touch mail order, they want to see what they're getting. So we've concentrated on distribution, getting them into the shops.' Apart from their own shop, they supply about 120 others: specialist-games shops, model-and-hobby shops, toy shops, some newsagents, even a stamp dealer whose son played a game which he thought marvellous so he stocked it. 'The argument for mail order is that you make more profits, but we're only interested in mail order for areas where there aren't any shops.'

The paste-up person looks after the magazine. It's for the players and includes playing aids as well as notices about new games. 'We used to publish this little handout and charge 10p for it; it cost us £50 and came out every two months. Suddenly we jumped to a professional magazine on glossy paper with decent artwork. It cost £500 and that was quite a gamble.'

The shop pays for itself. Being specialist, 'people know we're number one in the hobby. We get people coming from the continent and Scotland just to visit our shop. We have a few customers who come in regularly, they'll buy anything. There's one guy, a computer programmer, he's about eighteen, and he buys any new game. There's been a move away from war games to science fiction and it's created a fanatical following, bigger than anything that's happened in games before.'

Stephen J and his partner attempt to keep up with the new games but, inevitably, the business comes before the hobby. 'That's the crunch when you're doing something that you enjoy doing. You have to decide between the hobby and the business. If you're on in years, or feel secure in your work, you may concentrate on the hobby and get overtaken by somebody who puts the job first.

'It's up to us to keep pace with the games, but what we're both trying to do is more of the up-front stuff and leave the general administration to employees so we can go off and develop bigger things – like starting up new companies, new shops.' In 1979, with another person, they started a limited company dealing in miniatures: princesses, warriors . . . That began through somebody writing and saying 'he was fed up with university life and was going to work for a living. Soon after he wrote and said, "I've left, I'm all yours." We didn't take much notice but then he started up his own company and he seemed to have quite a bit of go about him; after a while he went freelance and eventually the three of us set up this company dealing in miniatures.'

Full-time

Income: B (£50 a week after tax plus occasional extras; 'it's the profits of the partnership plus what we pay ourselves as employees of the company, and we don't pay ourselves anything at the moment')

WHOLEFOOD WAREHOUSE

1980: The Wholefood Warehouse is an example of how an inspired idea – simple and sensible – happened to be in the right place at the right time. The idea was to supply wholefood – rice, flour, muesli, nuts, lentils, herbs, honey, beans – in medium sizes and at medium prices, thus filling the gap between the large wholesalers and the small retailers.

Nicholas S, proprietor, entrepreneur and organizer, started delivering food to Christiana, a commune in Copenhagen, after publishing *Alternative London* and *Alternative England and Wales*. He got to know the trade and to like the people in it. He enjoyed that kind of food, was looking for something new to do, and believed in food co-ops (as he saw it his potential customers) as not only a way of saving money but as a means of enabling people to do more for themselves.

As to the right time: it was the mid to late seventies when many people had been thoroughly awakened to the evils of white flour and sugar and the delights of muesli and home-baked bread. It was a time also when economies had to be made and a well-stocked larder of monochrome browns looked more appealing then any amount of fancy packaging. The place was also important: Covent Garden had been divested of its fruit and vegetable market and was fast turning into one of the most alive areas in London, full of independent businesses. Nicholas S had the freehold of a small warehouse there in Neal's Yard.

In November 1976 he set up shop. For the first few weeks business was slow, despite advertisements in the personal columns of *Time Out*, *Private Eye* and the *Observer*. Then the *Evening Standard* gave the shop a mention, which was followed by another in the *Observer*. Business boomed. One day, two months after opening, the shop took £1,000.

'People were streaming into the shop,' says Nicholas S. 'It didn't matter about it being hard to find, it's not passing trade, it's a specialist market. Originally, I thought I would only be staying six months and then handing over to someone else, but we got more and more busy and I got intrigued by ways of organization. What developed, since we didn't have room for many people, was a system whereby people worked for three days only, either Monday/Tuesday/Wednesday or Thursday/Friday/Saturday. The team of about five people did a lot of driving (because we fetch most of the stuff from wholesalers nearly every day), unloading, packing and serving in the shop, and cleaning (mainly jars). It could mean a twelve-hour day. Once a month we alternated shifts, one team worked for a continuous week – except Sunday – and the others got a whole week off.'

Employees got a percentage of the takings rather than a flat wage; this fluctuated but was generally around six and a half per cent, so that the team at the end of the week, when takings were more, got paid more. If someone did not turn up the others had to work harder and got paid more. Pay averaged between £60 and £80 a week, sometimes as low as £50 or as high as £100. This was net. The company paid the income tax – thus, as many people think, putting this tax properly in its place as a tax on production.

In addition, a duty manager, someone with more experience, worked from 10am to 6pm and got paid a flat salary. The duty manager did all the ordering, pricing and checking; it was his or her job to see that the shop ran well, to deal with customer complaints and the health inspector, to do the banking and count the money. At a later date, the job of shift leader developed. The shift leader did some of the jobs that the duty manager used to do, such as checking that the shelves were well stacked and that jars were not liable to fall over.

Nicholas S saw quite clearly that the Wholefood Warehouse was a specialist shop and that the way to make a go of it was to stock a limited number of lines: three sorts of rice, one grade of red beans, and so on. Prices must be reasonable – or low for the larger quantities. Everything on the price list must be in stock. 'You have to be reliable. If a food co-op is buying, you have to provide what you say you do.' He worked out a pricing structure, 'which I thought represented the true cost of selling the food. For each item it cost something because that item has to be lifted, it has to be rung up on the till. I put on a charge for each item of 10p, then a percentage which was fifteen per cent at the beginning, then ten per cent, then fifteen per cent because costs have gone up a lot. The philosophy behind the percentage is that it is money tied up, not just interest, it is something you might lose. Then 1p per pound weight is added and that's because the heavier the item the more work it is to handle. There is a packing charge for things we pack here (which is nearly everything) and that varies between 10p for those which are easy, like beans and rice, to the worst things, like Marmite, which is 50p. Dried fruit is 25p. The packing charge doesn't depend on size. The overall markup varies between twenty and ninety per cent, the largest percentage being on the smallest size of the most awkward thing to pack.' Honey, arriving in big drums, is poured into half-gallon jars.

At the beginning, Nicholas S tried for unusual bargains; but the poppyseed he bought from a bird-seed manufacturer turned out to be poor quality and sugar from the London sugar market was too dirty to sell. He now uses regular wholesalers for all his foodstuffs. Prices are keenly compared and there are 'no loyalties whatsoever, we drop somewhere if it gets more expensive. Our prices go up and down accordingly. If it's less than five per cent change we leave it.' Storage space is small compared to turnover.

The packing room is an essential part of the business. Situated immediately above the shop it also stores food. At one end there is a long packing trough lined with formica and divided across the middle. The trough holds two sacks at either end and is angled so that it is easy to shovel with scoops into the bags, which are then weighed and sealed with colour-coded ties. The colour is changed every two weeks to indicate old stock. The filled bags are put on a shelf behind; someone else then marks them for price, puts them in a crate and sends them down a chute to the shop below. It is economical in terms of time and energy and involves no noisy machines. Nicholas S thinks this kind of work is important: 'I feel very strongly that people should take responsibility for themselves and do a variety of work and not regard it as a lifetime's job but purely as an education – learning how to work.

'It's mostly manual work which I think is more rewarding because you are actually in touch with the goods. It is important that people get a chance to develop different sides of their personality, particularly doing those things which most middle-class people don't do, such as manual work: doing things carefully, seeing what needs to be done and working with other people as a group. All these are important and I think this place offers such opportunities. I've never thought people should stay here long: one of them has gone on to manage Ceres, one started an organic farm, some have gone to study, got other jobs, gone abroad.'

In 1977 Nicholas S bought a small building opposite and set up a bakery which has been very successful, paying back the setting-up costs in a year. A mill in the yard grinds flour and a dairy makes yoghurt and traditional soft English cheeses. Round the corner another shop sells coffee in bulk. All these businesses were originally financed by Nicholas S. and all are run independently of him and the Wholefood Warehouse.

In September 1979 Nicholas S left the running of the Wholefood Warehouse to Michael for a year. 'He's running it how he wants. Inevitably I don't like it very much. It's an unsatisfactory arrangement not having left altogether and not being in control.' The shift system has changed for a start, though to the customer it looks much as it has always done: solid timber shelving in the shop and armful-sized down-to-earth foodstuffs. At one time there was pressure to go into smaller sizes and luxury items, but 'people don't know what to ask for except what they've seen in the shop next door. If you're going to do anything original the last thing you do is stock what people ask for. There's a strong tendency to turn into the same place as everywhere else. You've got to do something different and I'm sure that it's the people who do something different and are convinced that it's a good idea who actually make a go of it.' Nicholas S has moved on to designing a range of stacking flowerpots for 'growing a garden up and along a wall'.

Full-time
Capital: Nicholas S already owned the premises
total cost for setting up shop (building work, fitting out, stock, wages, etc.) was below £20,000 ('since that is what I had – I expect I could have managed with £10,000')

the first truck cost £350 at auction and lasted two years; replacement cost £6,000

Income: Nicholas S's income: D (over £5,000; 'up until last year I was putting everything back into the other new shops and probably spent £2,000 on myself')

£60 to £80 a week on average for employees

Formal qualifications: none

Experience: mechanical-engineering skills, restoring houses, publishing books

Seven months later: 'Michael now wants to buy the business, which I am giving to Dartington beforehand so that the money goes to Dartington who will spend it on a project of my choice (probably a magazine to put inventors in touch with manufacturers). Michael is making a lot of changes – checkouts like supermarkets, more variety of expensive stock in small sizes, less big sizes, small jars, deliveries, two vans. I believe his plan is eventually to move the bulk business and make Neal's Yard more "boutiquey".'

CHAPTER FOUR

House & Home

HOME DESIGN

1976: Not many people see three years' work disappear in three-quarters of an hour, but it happened to Paul O. He was also deprived of a home when the house he was working on – replumbing, rewiring and refurbishing – caught fire in 1970. With no financial resources, he decided to make a temporary living by hiring himself out as a 'repairer, rearranger and maker of bits and pieces'. He has been doing this ever since. All his work is one-off designs, whether for the furnishings and fittings of a kitchen or a scheme for a foldaway bed. People come to him with their problems, very often problems of space. A typical problem can go like this: two people live in a one-room flat with alley kitchen and tiny bathroom. They have vast quantities of books, records and three cats. At the moment it looks like a scruffy bedsit with planks thrown against the wall and curtains pulled across the bed. How can it be turned into an attractive flat with twice as much space to play in? Solution: design and make furniture which folds, tucks and disappears into the wall when it is not needed.

After time spent as an engineering and industrial-design student and researcher into laboratory equipment, Paul O decided to become a practical man and volunteered to improve his parents' house, stage by stage, learning as he went, if they would agree to pay him a minimum wage. To their credit they accepted. 'I did that for seven years,' he says, 'not all the time, but gradually I built up a full working knowledge of carpentry and all the rest of it and I was responsible for everything in the house, all the fittings and furnishings.' It was, as he says, 'extremely tentative at the beginning, I had very few tools. I didn't have a plane and I borrowed a saw. Now I have a couple of hundred quid's worth of tools, though nothing very glamorous.' He bought, cheaply, some shop counters for sinks and storage units. 'It's a good way for anybody to start, by converting existing pieces of furniture,' he says, 'because you are relieved of the problems of designing from the bottom up for structural strength and for getting everything square.'

While serving his apprenticeship, as it were, Paul O improved the house he was living in and then came the fire. He has never been out of work since; he makes enough money to live on but not enough 'to buy myself out of favours. If I had a bit of capital I would buy a workshop instead of having to saw wood in the garden.' His pricing is partly at fault, he admits. 'I get interested in jobs and I get ideas and they work out but take three times as long. At the end you realize you were four weeks instead of two, that it cost not a couple of quid chasing after this and that but seven or eight and you're really fagged out. The job is done, the person is happy and they've willingly accepted a ten to twenty per cent increase because they know it's good value. But they won't accept a hundred per cent increase.' Part of the answer is to simplify the design so that 'you have a modular way of making things instead of completely comprehensive all-over speculation every time you take on a new piece of work'.

When he first meets a prospective customer, Paul O discusses the work and 'asks them what they're prepared to spend, what they've seen in the shops and what seems worthwhile expenditure'. Details and basic scale drawings go in a folder and the materials are bought or picked up from previous work. At that stage he takes fifty per cent in advance from the customer. Only once has somebody not paid him. Apart from individual customers, Paul O has worked as a subcontractor for an architect and vows never to do it again. 'It looked profitable when it was offered several years ago,' he says, 'but so many things did not run according to plan. I would turn up to find that the place didn't have any floors and I would have to find a useful way of killing time and there is no useful way. This is where I score when I'm working on my own, because I do the plumbing and wiring and everything.'

Nine months later: For the last four months Paul O has been working on a £2,000 kitchen and, in the process, discovered a new way of pricing his work. Instead of basing his price on time and materials (i.e. what it costs him), he estimated on the price of an equivalent ready-made kitchen (i.e. what it would otherwise cost his customer to buy). This method benefits him financially and is considered just all round.

Full-time
Capital: none
  tools worth about £200
  back garden for sawing and hammering
  van essential
Income: B
Formal qualifications: engineering and industrial design

1980: Paul O moved into a basement flat with a workshop. Above is the kitchen he worked on, to which he is still adding the finishing touches. 'The kitchen became protracted and stretched over a period of more than three years, though most of it was done in three months. In the end it will probably work out at twice the original budget. Philip was fairly easy-going about it, so I used it as a project for trying out everything I thought was relevant. I've also done other renovation work here: new window frames, a large and fancy front door, bits of rewiring, levelling floors . . .

'I treat most things as an experiment, which means that you're almost inevitably working for private people and not companies. If you get involved in working everything as a one-off then you have to work for people who are one-offs as well – people with large incomes who think it is rather fun to have you fooling around making something for them. It's impossible for me to make a simple chest of drawers which competes in price with anything you can buy from a discount warehouse.'

Full-time
Income: 'Gone up marginally' – he charges £4 to £5 an hour
free flat and workshop
Tools: total investment about £500 to include benches
van pays its way by doing removals

DECORATING

1976: Many actors find themselves out of work at one time or another and David K was no exception. As a student he worked as a decorator for his father, simply because 'I needed to support myself with a certain amount of freedom and without the restrictions of being in a normal job'. He has worked in this way for the last ten years, finding clients through personal recommendation and picking up experience and new techniques as he went along. 'I started off doing painting and decorating,' he says, 'and then it extended to paper-hanging. I even specialize in that; hanging a lot of the modern wallpapers. the vinyl and foil ones, fabrics and silks.' Another speciality is intricate painting and working with gold leaf; one job was sub-contracting to paint cornices in Buckingham Palace. 'Lots of people try their hand at decorating,' he says. 'Materials are simpler and everything becomes easy and few people specialize. So if you do specialize invariably you will corner that end of the market.'

David K charges £12 a day for his labour ('I can remember when it was £5; every six months I review it again'), plus the cost of materials and expenses. One job does not always follow straight on from another and he admits that he would be better off if he worked for an employer, but 'I have an aversion to it in every way. The nearest I've come to it is in sub-contracting, when the standard of work is taken out of your hands, what you do and the way in which it is done. If you're lucky enough to work for somebody who does demand good standards and is well organized, it's fine, but usually it isn't like that, you waste a lot of your time, whereas it's only natural to get on with it and do it.'

One of the most important parts of the job, he says, is finding out exactly what people want – and that isn't always easy. 'Invariably you will be given a magazine and told, "I want that," but if you have a little semi-detached you can't turn it into an Italian villa. Often it is a matter of people wanting to superimpose something that is totally unrealistic and not seeing the potential of what they really have.' A house is also a home, dear to the owner's heart, and many hearts want it to be the same as it always has been, regardless. In the end 'you can't impose your taste,' says David K, 'you have to remember that you're really the servant of the people you're working for'. Nevertheless he is often called upon to give advice. Experience in stage design helps: 'I used to work in austere companies so you had to create the maximum effect with the minimum amount. You realize how easily, by introducing one colour or item, you can completely create an atmosphere, often very simply.'

Working on his own, David K maintains the minimum of equipment and outlay – just a car with a roof-rack. He has thought of expanding, 'employing people, with a yard and all the rest of it, but then you lose contact, you're an administrator and rely on other people's skills. And the bigger you are the harder you fall. When you're a one-mand band you haven't got much to lose – but you don't stand much chance of growth either.'

At the moment he is just about to grow. In a new project getting off the ground David K will be working alongside another interior designer. He will be employed for a few days at a time, lending his practical experience to complement the other's technical and drawing abilities. 'It's a natural development,' he says. 'At times I get browned off continually painting people's bedrooms and I would like to do something with more scope.' Two designers, he reckons, can cover far more ground working together than working separately. 'You can only be in one place at any one time,' he says, 'either travelling round jobs in progress or researching them or at the drawing board. If there is just one person he has to be on site a lot of the time which keeps him right away from his drawing board. With two of you a much greater volume of work can be maintained.'

Nine months later: 'The design project didn't materialize,' says David K, 'because there wasn't enough work to keep the two of us going. After I picked up the threads again I had lots of offers for decorating work. What I'm finding now is that do-it-yourself is fading out a bit; people have tried their own decorating and the results aren't good enough. My prices have also gone up to £13 or £14 a day and nobody seems to mind that. I think they accept that costs and materials are always going up.'

Full-time
Capital: none

tools (including ladder) worth about £200
van or car essential, with roof-rack
no separate premises

Income: C
Formal qualifications: none
Experience: in stage design

1980: 'It's essential when working for yourself to start on a business footing. I started decorating for friends and that's when things often go wrong; I repeat for old customers who are used to the old prices and will argue about rates. The only way out of that situation is to put your foot down.

'When pricing you have got to account for the whole year: you can lose a month with sickness and holidays. Each week you have to earn more if you're just to keep up. This year I will turn over £5,000 – which is the best so far. I've got three children and I rent this flat very cheaply. There's no way I could afford to buy anything round here, which is where my work is.'

From time to time other people join David K – mainly for decorating, although he also works with a sculptor who carves in stone. Both of them can carve in wood and David K also does some carpentry, such as making floors and wardrobes. He is investigating the possibilities of making relief mouldings, surrounds and brackets from plaster moulds, mainly for renovating Victorian houses but also for modern flats. 'In the theatre we built everything from plaster moulds. You can carve a figure and take as many casts as you want.'

Despite hard times, David K has found that people are prepared to pay for skill. 'In the sixties it was the cult of the amateur and do-it-yourself. By the time people get to buying their second house and especially their third house, they don't want to go through the hassle of doing it up themselves so they get somebody in to do it. What is often not realized is that decorating adds enormously to the value of a house. At the end of last year I decorated a seven-bedroom house. The owner bought it for £50,000. My bill for decorating was £2,000. Altogether he probably spent £10,000 and could put it on the market for £85,000.'

David K sees himself very much as the local decorator. 'I'm inundated with work; all my clients are living on my doorstep, it doesn't pay me to go further afield than Kew or Barnes. In the old days every community had a local builder, with a hand-cart, and he served the community. That's the way it should be. It's less efficient in every way to spend time and money travelling.'

Full-time
Income: D (£5,000 + ; £20 to £30 a day plus materials)

PLUMBING
1976: Bernard D used to help his father in the holidays and when he left school, he set out to become a plumber. He worked firstly for his father and then as an 'improver' for another firm while he took City and Guilds examinations in plumbing, heating and ventilation. After about seven years he rejoined his father, doing small jobs such as sink units, wash basins and bathrooms. When his father retired, he became self-employed with lots of misgivings. Doubts were unfounded. Finding work is no problem; he is booked up two or three months in advance, one job leading to another, all within a five-mile radius. Paperwork is a major bugbear, that and organizing a working life where he may do many jobs in one week and never know in advance how long each one is going to take. 'I've got a diary which is really phone messages,' he says, 'but I never put down "Mr Smith is going to take four days." I used to do that and it never worked out. So now I put, "Wednesday I've got to go out and I think it will take a day." So I book Wednesday and it might take me to Thursday but I'll still be busy Thursday whether this job overlaps or not. So I don't commit myself every day. I'll commit myself to two, maybe three, jobs a week.' The rest of the time is spent on emergency work: the 'water is dripping through the ceiling' variety and other quick jobs, such as . . . 'A woman rang up tonight; her radiators aren't working. She's an old customer so I should help her. It could take half a day, it might take an hour.' In these circumstances forward planning is difficult. 'I should write down, "Mr Smith is thinking about a shower in six weeks," and then look up two weeks in advance to see what my work commitments are.'

Most of Bernard D's customers, about eighty per cent, come to him through other customers. He also keeps his name in the Yellow Pages – his only advertising. 'Unless you want to expand a lot you really shouldn't have to advertise,' he says. Most people ring in the evening or at any rate after half past three in the afternoon, when his wife gets in. The pair of them are sometimes jumping up and down all evening answering the phone. He accepts jobs up to about £500 worth of work, estimating for the larger ones and charging by the hour for the smaller ones. It works out at about £3 an hour.

Apart from the business side, plumbing suits Bernard D very well, 'though it can get a bit boring if you're in an empty house; you end up talking to yourself. But I don't have to clock in; I can start at seven and end at three o'clock without asking anybody.' The main thing about being a good plumber, he says, 'is that you do a reasonable job for a reasonable price. The price is not as important as the work you do.' What about those maverick plumbers who charge you £10 if they so much as replace a tap washer? 'Three-quarters of the stories I've heard,' he says, 'it's been the emergency service that's at fault. It really depends who is driving the van that day whether you get a proper plumber at work.' He tells a horrific story: somebody 'called in an emergency plumber because her cold water wasn't running very well. He said he would have to connect it to the mains because bigger pressure would push the blockage out. He connected the mains to the hot-water tank which burst and brought the ceiling down. Then he told her it was going to break anyway. It cost about £170 and all it probably needed was a bit of wire poking down the pipe; the plumber didn't know what he was doing.' So what is the best way of learning what to do? 'I found I learnt far more working for a plumber than I did at school,' he says. 'Unless you're planning big projects you don't need to know half the calculations I was taught. The do-it-yourself magazines are quite helpful on the theory side, but you can't beat practical work.'

Full-time
Capital: basic tools cost about £100
  car or van essential
  no separate premises
Income: C
Formal qualifications: from City and Guilds
Experience: previous employment

1980: Bernard D hated doing the paperwork when he worked for himself. He found that he promised too much, got behind, worked late, and his family suffered. So, with a sigh of relief, for the next eighteen months he will be working for a friend while he plumbs in sixteen flats. 'He'll be the guv'nor,' he says, 'though I shall have a lot to say about the design and how things should work.' And a change of work could help him when he returns to self-employment. As he puts it, 'I may learn better ways of running a business. I shall be getting a regular wage and shan't have to worry about paying the bills – though money was never a problem. I still do odd jobs for regular clients – one or two evenings a week or on Saturday mornings.'

Will being employed change his attitude towards the work?

'I don't think so, I always wanted to do that little bit more. If something went wrong with my plumbing, say, within six months of doing it, I would return and fix it free of charge and I think any good plumber would do the same.'

Full-time
Income: £5 an hour, which works out closer to £3 an hour for extended jobs, plus overheads
1980 resolution: 'Don't make promises!

BUILDING

1976: Throughout the upheavals of the sixties building boom and into the stringent seventies the small local builder was often a perennial amongst the fast-fading annuals. Derek E belongs to this breed, although he has only been working as a builder for the last eighteen months. He had always been a do-it-yourself man and learnt the basics of building by hiring the village builder to renovate his own house and working as his labourer. Then, as a farmer, he did his own building, but it wasn't until he went to Yorkshire that he joined up with two others and started taking on outside jobs. 'The difficult thing is making a start,' he says. 'We found postcards in newsagents' windows the best thing, but then you do a couple of jobs and the news spreads very quickly by word-of-mouth.'

They found a market in renovating cheap, dilapidated property, 'mainly bought by young people. It needed an inside loo and bathroom, walls knocked down, that sort of thing.' With a van and roof-rack and about £200 worth of tools accumulated over the years, Derek E is equipped to tackle brick-laying, concreting, plastering, decorating and plumbing. 'The ideal', he says, 'is to have two or three blokes – one, say, a joiner, one a plumber and another an electrician. In any case there are quite a lot of jobs that are difficult to do single-handed.' Now that he has moved to a community in Suffolk, Derek E is working with a joiner there. 'You try to diversify your skills as much as you can,' he says. 'I've taught Chris to plaster, which he had never done and never thought he could do. Plastering is a thing which has a fair amount of mystique attached to it. Again, I would like to know more about electronics.' Their first big job is on a house in a low-cost housing area in Ipswich. It will need a new roof and their boards will hang on the scaffolding for all to see – and perhaps bring in new work.

Another way of finding work is to link with an architect, as Derek E did in Yorkshire: 'He got in with the local Pakistani population and when they said could he recommend a builder, he would suggest us.'

As well as familiarity with planning laws a builder needs to know the building regulations, 'which vary in parts of the country. I've only just discovered,' he says, 'that in the next district you can't use brass fittings any longer, they've got to be gunmetal because of the composition of the water.'

Derek E lives quite simply and has few administrative overheads. If the two of them took on a £1,000 job it might take a month or six weeks, for which they each earn about £12 a day. The cost of the materials is a heavy outlay, although 'you can arrange with the customer to make progress payments which at least cover the cost of your materials.' Estimating, he says, is the most skilful part of the job. 'If you quoted to do a job on the basis that it would take a month and you hit snags and it takes you two months your earnings are going to be half of what you expected. It's always a relief when you finish on time.'

Building work can be highly competitive. 'There is a big temptation to cut things too fine,' says Derek E. 'If you're employing a couple of chaps you've get to meet their wage bill every week, so you're desperate to keep them busy. If there are two or three of you working together and you're not earning anything you're prepared not to draw anything out. I think you ought to warn people not to embark alone on this sort of thing until they've had a fair bit of experience, because you can leave yourself wide open to all sorts of mistakes.'

Seven months later: 'There are four of us now,' says Derek E. 'We've been joined by two learners and work is going pretty well.

We had a slack period at the end of the summer, but now we're booked up six months ahead. It's all work with private houses, locally: extensions, roofing, brick-laying, that sort of thing. As people get to know about us we get more work, some of it in the village.'

Full-time
Capital: £200 worth of tools
  van essential, with roof-rack
  no separate premises
Income: B
Formal qualifications: none

1980: In 1977 Derek E moved to rural Dumfriesshire and tried to establish himself locally. It wasn't easy. 'For much of the time I was single-handed and had not realized how often one needs another pair of hands. I have been convinced of the truth of the saying that two people can do three times the work of one person. Also the area is sparsely populated, economically disadvantaged and competition for work is strong.'

He persevered, however, and prospects now look brighter. A friend from Yorkshire joined him and they hope to recruit more people (at least seven), form a building co-operative and register it with the Industrial Common Ownership Movement. 'The idea of worker co-operatives is very much in the air here, as a possible answer to the general economic and social depression, and successful examples have appeared in quite different fields. With their emphasis on self-determination, initiative and responsibility they have an important contribution to make in restoring morale and self-respect, which are much needed in a depressed area.'

Technically Derek E has diversified his skills and has mastered domestic electrical installation. 'I have also tried to develop some expertise in the more ecologically sensitive aspects of building; not so much aero-generators and water-power, as insulation, double-glazing and the installation of wood-burning stoves and cookers. I would hope to see a big increase in this part of our work.'

FURNITURE RENOVATION

1976: Sue M has a husband, three children, another on the way and a back room stuffed full of furniture in the process of being stripped.

She enjoys working with wood; one of her previous activities was picture framing, but even more satisfying is taking in a 'tatty old chest of drawers covered with layers of paint and bringing it up a lovely mellow colour'. She and her husband, Bruce, began stripping furniture as a hobby. About a year ago, she bought a couple of kitchen chairs from a junk yard and, when they were sanded and polished, Bruce asked, 'Why don't you sell them?' Sue M picked up a chest of drawers off a rag-and-bone man in the street and rather laboriously stripped it; then, saving up her family allowance until she had £30, she bought another chest of drawers, three or four chairs and two tables.

'It was the beginning of the summer,' she says, 'and I worked outside. I put an advert in the local paper. The first person who came bought two chairs and wanted two more as well as a dining-room table. She paid me for the chairs which gave me the money for the table.' A local upholsterer also came and invited Sue M to sell her furniture in a monthly Saturday market, to be organized on the forecourt of his shop. 'That was the greatest impetus of all,' she says. 'I never worked so hard in my life. On the day, we loaded up the furniture at nine o'clock and somebody was already waiting for us. I sold everything that day plus the things half finished and ordered.' The upholsterers also had a good day, and Sue M now works mostly towards the next month's sale.

The furniture which Sue M likes is basic English, often pine or walnut, the chairs of beech with elm seats. The biggest demand, she finds, is for chests of drawers and seamen's chests. 'What is so appealing about it', she says, 'is that it is so plain and simple you couldn't improve on it in any way. Most of it is a good deal better than the modern furniture.' Bruce M explains further. 'I think there's a reaction against plastic stuff so more people want better quality furniture such as we like and provide.'

At the beginning, Sue M used to 'go out in the car, take the kids and look for stuff – but it's very time-consuming'. Now she buys from an antique dealer who does house clearance and has introduced her to other dealers and shops. All her supplies of furniture come this way. Over a period of time she has learnt to judge the quality of the wood lying underneath the paint, what will reward stripping and what is best forgotten. Back home, the furniture is taken outside to a convenient concrete yard, stripped, hosed down and left to dry. Occasionally, pieces get sent off for professional stripping, but 'there are so many people,' she says, 'who plonk the stuff in, turn up the thermostat, leave it for a couple of days and it is ruined'.

Sanding and polishing follow on. Sometimes an otherwise good piece of furniture needs repairing and Bruce and Sue M carry out small repairs. Handles and other fittings are often missing or need replacing and Sue M scours local shops to find the right sort. Files are stacked on her shelves: records of where to get supplies, records of 'shops and what they're selling and how much their prices are. This is an invaluable compendium,' she says. Selling prices are fairly uniform. 'A chest of drawers will always cost £25; if you buy one with unusual handles it will be £28 and so on; but you never get anything less than £25.'

Nine months later: Sue M was in hospital for seven weeks before the baby was born. During that time her eldest son managed the Saturday market, her husband bought some furniture and dealers kept pieces back for her. Now, four months later, she is carrying on as before with some useful publicity from the local newspaper. 'Before I had the baby,' she says, 'I was determined to keep going. My only worry was that I might not be able to, but I find that I can. I'm also thinking of having a shop, perhaps one at the end of the road, or of going in with someone else to sell my stuff.'

Part-time
Capital: £30 for first stock
  storage space and yard
  car or van essential
  family assistance
Income: A
Formal qualifications: none

1980: Sue M found her shop (see page 71).

STEREO REPAIR/WINDMILLS
1976: Olaf U is living in a community of thirty adults and fifteen children with his wife and small son. He repairs stereo equipment which he collects from an electrical shop and brings back to a tiny 'laboratory' bristling with knobs, cables and apparatus. Then, restored to health, he returns them to the shop. He charges £2 an hour, which is enough to support himself and his family.

Ever since he was a child, Olaf U has been interested in electrical equipment – especially stereos. After university and working on Saturdays in a workshop, he set up on his own. He spread the word amongst his friends and advertised in *Time Out*, but now most of his work comes through the shop and he can take it away and 'give it a full test and check it over properly'. The other alternative is to 'go round with a screwdriver and a little volt meter and say, "We'll fix that up in no time," which doesn't encourage the customer to feel at all confident.'

After eight or nine years, Olaf U says he knows less than when he started; this can't be true, but it is a reminder of how quickly new products come on to the market and 'it's helpful to read magazines and do your own *Which?* research,' he says. 'In any case people ask you, so you need to know.' For somebody starting up, basic equipment costs about £100 and is sufficient for most stereos. Olaf U points out that no two problems are quite the same: 'You may find that you can't do the first one, or the second, and by the third you wonder, "Am I any good at all?" ' Persistence pays off. If it doesn't, the recalcitrant machine can always be handed over to another, more experienced person with little lost except a touch of pride. Once skills are established they become easier to sell. 'If I was starting again,' says Olaf U, 'I would do it with one other person who is commercially presentable and who would go to shops and say, "We'll take all your repair work, we'll charge you and you can charge your customers whatever you like; we'll guarantee the work and we'll do it inside a week," and we'll take all your troubles from you in effect. That is how I would do it. The chap who is best at talking is not necessarily the best at fixing the amp.'

While at first one may have to take anything offered, choosing the type of work preferred is surely the cherry on top of the self-employed cake. Olaf U suffers, he says, from a personal inability to say 'no'. 'I've spent a lot of time running around after small jobs which don't pay very well. Inexpensive equipment is sometimes hardly worth repairing, whereas somebody with hundreds of pounds' worth will pay to get it working properly.' People get very fussy about their stereos and his work has led Olaf U into swampy regions, as he explains: 'When people get quite neurotic about their stereos it's not just a hi-fi – it's their little baby with its problems. They buy something else and it's not quite what they want so they buy something else. It's not rational at all. There are a few people who sit and listen to the music, and for those it is fun to work, but the others are cases of "I think my volume control knob is wobbly; I'll have a new amp because of it," and that's not fun any more.'

Olaf U is looking for other areas of work. He and others in the community, including Derek E (see page 94), are investigating solar-roof heating which is already commercially viable and looks set for the future. One other project, along the same lines, is the erection of windmills for generating electricity. They have already put up a windmill for a self-sufficient doctor living in a windy part of Norfolk. The windmills are sold in kit form by Conservation Tools and Technology, but even so 'it's a bit complicated,' says Olaf U. 'There are two control panels and you have to fit together unusual bits and pieces, find the right sort of cables.' The kits are quite expensive, though eventually they pay for themselves. It is still early days, but as far as Olaf U is concerned it is a long-term project.

Seven months later: 'We are getting more work installing windmills,' says Olaf U. 'I have had a preliminary site inspection and customers' estimates for four or more windmills including one local one. I make useful little gadgets which are not in the CTT kit. We have also installed solar panels for a private swimming pool in Hendon, though it was a long way to go and we hardly made any money from it.'

Part-time
Capital: £100 for basic equipment (Olaf U's stereo repair equipment is worth about £2,000)
essentials are volt meter £10, oscilloscope £25 and signals generator (home-made)
car useful for collecting stereo equipment
no separate premises but small laboratory area
Income: A
Formal qualifications: electronics degree
Experience: previous part-time employment

1980: Olaf U spends his time installing windmills and making bits and pieces to supplement the CTT kits. He also repairs existing windmills, mends stereos for friends and does building and plumbing locally. He still finds it difficult to say 'no'.

'In principle the work I do now is new. The windmills are experimental and there is enough new stuff to keep me happy. I go all over the country with the windmills – I'm just off to deliver parts for a new windmill in Scotland. It might seem glamorous sometimes; I put up a windmill for the Prime Minister of Ireland off the west coast of Ireland and we went there by helicopter. It's demanding work and sometimes I think, "My God, what have I done?" when something goes wrong and it might have been my fault. All it needs is a bolt not to be tightened properly on a windmill and a blade disappears because it is turning too fast.'

The Natural Energy Centre acts as an agent for makers of windmills and puts clients in contact with Olaf U. Windmills are clearly going to be one of the energy tools of the future, but for the moment there has been no great take-off. In any case, Olaf U says he would like a job: 'I enjoy taking charge of things,' he says, 'but I would consider working for someone else just to take the responsibility off my shoulders. When you're on your own you haven't got fixed limits and people ask you for things and you want to be helpful and you let yourself in for something you didn't want. By most people's standards I earn peanuts; I'm not liable for tax that's how little I earn.'

Unusually, Olaf U says he doesn't want more money. It's not an easy dilemma for him to resolve, the dilemma of what work to take up: 'I haven't come across anything else I want to do, but I do know that I want to simplify the whole thing. Too much experimental work leads to too many sleepless nights.'

Full-time
Income: B

CHAPTER FIVE

Children & Teaching

NURSERY SCHOOL

1980: Caring for children, says Christine U, is more than letting them run around doing what they want and more than teaching them the ABC. 'It's a matter of developing human potential, to take care that they are being taught to be a complete human being.' Her nursery school, run on Montessori lines, has been attempting this for four years.

Swiss-born, Christine U trained with the Maria Montessori Training Organisation from 1970 to 1971. After a year's practical teaching she was qualified in the Montessori method and able to open her own school. The Montessori Society has certain standards for recognizing schools: there must be at least one qualified person for thirty children plus the required teaching apparatus.

When the children arrive in the morning they are shown how to take off their coat, undo their shoes, put on their slippers. They are also shown how to get out their work, how to do it and how to put it away. Christine U emphasizes that this is an important step. 'They do pouring and polishing, they do cleaning, things that a mother would do around the house. All the equipment they use is cut to their own size so they have tiny bottles and dusters. It's all very neatly kept and they put it on a mat so they can perform the activity from beginning to end in a very neat fashion.'

The children are then introduced to what is called sensorial apparatus – equipment designed to use their senses. 'Children take a natural delight in looking and listening, tasting and feeling. For example, there are sound boxes – two sets of six wooden cylinders, six with red tops and six with blue tops. You show the child one cylinder and you shake it and it makes a rattle and you take out the next cylinder with the same coloured top and it makes a slightly different sound. Then you say, "Let's find its partner." This attention creates a marvellous sense of absorption in the classroom.' There are exercises for all five senses. The children are also taught to read, starting with I-Spy which leads on to 'feeling' the sandpaper letters and sounding them and then recognizing the letter when it is held up. A skilful reading and writing scheme follows. The same approach is used for numbers. They are also introduced to the world in which they live through geography, the world of animals and plants, music and art.

Behind all this activity lies a powerful idea. 'Montessori was not primarily interested in academic results. She was really interested in creating a society that lives in peace and she felt that people who are fulfilled are people who are able to live in harmony. She says that every child will naturally work and will never try to cut down on any activity of life, in the way that a grown-up does, for the end result. The child always works in order to perfect himself. You only need to watch a child at the beach: how many times does he fill his pail and tip it up, do it again and again? It is never the same activity, there is always something happening, a sense of achievement.'

Christine U started her school at home when her eldest child was two and a half. She felt that he needed company and 'was keen that he should be taught and spend the morning in a constructive fashion. I found it a little bit of a lonely task with one child (in fact I had another of eighteen months). So I thought why not get other children together and then, having the training, use it? So it started with a neighbour's child and my own two for the first three months and then I put an ad. up in the Post Office and got somebody who had just come back from Oman.' The back room was used for teaching and materials and the breakfast room for milk and biscuits and washing up and scrubbing and clay and painting.

When the number of children at the school increased to eight, Christine U had to look for somebody to help her. 'I didn't at the time have the money to pay someone else to come in and help. I was relying on goodwill and it seemed difficult to find somebody regularly for the conditions that I could offer.' For reasons of space she was limited to eight children as she 'wanted to stay at home because of my small children. One does not want to leave in the morning if they have a cold or are a bit off-colour or if your child is in the first year of school.'

Now, however, she is holding her school in a local hall. 'I had a lot of enquiries from parents and thought I would take a hall. I found this one quite by chance. The procedures are that you have to contact the social services first, the fire brigade officer follows and you put in for planning permission. This particular hall used to have a nursery group so the permissions were all ready. So I was told, "Start tomorrow if you wish." As a word of warning, it can take up to three months.'

Christine U has twenty-one children and two helpers, whose children also attend. Now that she has more room she is expanding the apparatus. But it all costs money. 'There's a lot of expense on educational apparatus, painting paper, paste and you tend to buy books and puzzles. Any good puzzle is about £3 these days and a book is about £3. You have to pay for the hall and there is also the cost of insuring it.'

Even while working at home you need to go through the social services, says Christine U. 'They are concerned that there is enough equipment, that the space is right, your qualifications are there: it helps to be a nursery nurse or teacher but you don't have to hold a specific training for that age group. I think they want to see that you are a responsible person.'

Is it work that any mother can do?

'It depends,' she says. 'If they thought you were around to earn some money and that was the easiest way to do it you wouldn't get permission. If they are aware that you are genuinely interested in education and care of the children it is worthwhile trying.'

There is clearly a demand for this service. 'People are concerned that their children are educated, that they can mix and be in a constructive environment. They like the aspect that there is discipline, the child is working and there is a general order to the morning; the child really learns something, not in a forced way but by taking the child as a guide. You move as fast as the child will move, not at your own pace.

'The ideal behind my work is that one day the mothers will be able to do the job that I am doing with their children. So my work will not be necessary. Because I do feel that there is no better teacher for a child than its mother.'

Part-time (mornings in term-time)
Capital: £400 four years ago for apparatus, chairs and tables
  £1,000 loan from the bank, more recently, for new apparatus and cupboards
  no separate premises at first; then local hall
  £17 per morning/week for each helper
Income: £70 per child per term (minus expenses)
Formal qualifications: Montessori Diploma
Experience: two years' teaching in Montessori school

TEACHING
i. Singing and music
1976: Any student can have a hard time after leaving college; all of a sudden the wraps are whisked away, and with little knowledge of the commercial world and less experience of earning a livelihood it can be a daunting business. A very few jet to the very top of their profession; some never try, but most put on their boots and settle down for a long haul. Rosemary B is one of these. She is a good pianist but, on her own admission, not good enough to play solo. Coming from New Zealand on an Arts Council bursary she studied at the Royal Academy for three years and then found herself without a job and with nowhere to go. 'I hadn't planned at all,' she says. 'You're not encouraged to if you're artistic, you're not supposed to worry about things like that; your great talent should see you through, something should come down on strings from heaven.' It didn't.

Fortified by twelve hours piano teaching at a school, just enough to live on, Rosemary B started giving one or two private lessons. 'I was living a nomadic life at the time,' she says, 'because I could never keep down any lodgings for long; I was carting this piano about. It was the noise really. The problem of a musician. You're too much in someone's private house unless they want it.' Then, about a year after she left college, Rosemary B began to play for an ILEA evening class. Her total earnings were £19 a week. Now, six years later, she gives twenty hours a week private coaching (and two or three children's piano lessons) at £2.50 an hour and spends another twenty hours playing for young aspiring professional singers in ILEA classes, principally Opera Viva. What has happened in the six years?

'I had to live so I had to work,' she says. 'I was moving in several different directions at once and not knowing where I was going, and I was green and as soft as a bag of sponges about money. It seemed demeaning to one's art to be selling it for money and yet one wasn't good enough to perform. I should have realized that if I wasn't good enough to perform I was doing what was my level, teaching, but it took me a while to accept that. There was an Indian philosopher, once, who said, "You can only teach people what is already inside them." I think that in the performing arts to be told something is not very useful. What you've got to do is inspire the person to a level of response where they start to do things that are in them. Sometimes it's valid to say, "Do a *crescendo* on that note," because you can see that they have the germ of the idea in their mind and haven't dared to do it. I prefer to say, "It would be nice to do that . . ." so we arrive at it between us.

'With singers it's very interesting, because every voice has its own quality. You're not teaching them singing, they've got all the notes; you've got to start with the quality of that particular voice. It's absolutely fascinating because it's always different; sometimes I feel that I had a good session with so-and-so, I really got a response from them, I lifted them up to a level they wouldn't have got to on their own. That's what it is, you're really behind them, not in front, so they in the end go forward themselves . . . that must be the aim of all good teaching – that you're behind the students, propelling them forwards. In the end they'll have enough momentum in their own legs and they'll go away from you. It's very like being a good mother, being a good teacher. I've told you that great teaching is the best thing that can happen to art because it will raise the level of performance. Performers will teach each other, but if there are one or two to whom the top singers can go and learn something, they're the most valuable people in the singing profession. They're the ones who keep the art alive.'

Eight months later: 'Well, nothing very much has changed except that the ILEA are paying more for Opera Viva which is nice.'

Full-time
Capital: none
no separate premises but room for piano
Income: C
Formal qualifications: from Royal Academy of Music

1980: 'If a prestige good job came up I would take it, because of the prestige. I've got to the stage where, if you haven't done a stint with Covent Garden or Glyndebourne, people think you're no good. You have to work with a professional opera house sooner or later – and I do have that ambition. I would like to be somebody who is called on to coach in languages – I've got French, German and Italian.'

Rosemary B's career has not stood still, though she sees it more as a vocation than in terms of money. 'I gave up Opera Viva in June 1979; I had been with it for eight years and it felt too long; I was doing administrative work and that felt wrong. It was quite a lot of money – £40 a week for nine hours, thirty-four weeks of the year . . . I still work at Morley College, nine hours as a coach repetiteur, purely as an opera coach.

'Morley is my bread and butter. I try to keep my employment level up so I'll have my insurance stamps paid and get the benefits of an employee. I do twenty hours opera and *lieder* coaching at home; no piano lessons, I never really wanted to do that.'

Slowly but surely, Rosemary B is making a name for herself. Conductors ask for her; opera companies want to work with her; she is assisting with recordings and teaching vocal repertoire and accompaniment on an occasional basis at the Royal College. Recently, she was recommended for the *World Who's Who of Women* and invited for the *International Who's Who in Music* ('so I must be getting famous!').

Paying £10 a week for rent and rates, Rosemary B says she can afford to be idealistic. 'I charge £4 an hour for coaching. When I've been asked to do something I never ask about the money, I ask myself whether I want to do the job and think about the money after. That's why I see music as a vocation, which not everybody does now. I want what I do to be good and if somebody really wants me to work with them that matters far more than the money. If it's good I feel happy. The money mustn't come first – though it mustn't be forgotten.'

Full-time
Income: D

ii. Dance
1980: Roger T teaches outside an institutionalized system; as a teacher of dance, he attempts to teach from his own experience and within the classical tradition. The two, one an independence and the other a connection, are linked in the dance. This is how he sees it: 'The tradition of teaching dance was that the dancers became the teachers. But in this institutionalized age people like to have a system and think they can produce the same product; they create a system, institutionalize it and teachers teach within that. So many teachers teaching within the arts, certainly in dancing, are not what one would call independent. Art has always been taught by artists who have passed on their experience and craft.' Teaching within a system is particularly dangerous, he says, because it produces teachers who teach teachers – and none of them may be dancers. It's like being taught to drive a car by someone who has never driven one. The result is mechanical and lifeless, a superimposition – of that he feels certain.

Teaching within a system or teaching from the tradition is an important distinction for Roger T; it is all seen within the dance. That is the most important thing. 'Dance is a great expression of joy, a great song of praise. The work is not to teach the dancer but to remove the impediments. You've got to see a like nature, a like response, and help them to find that for themselves. It's the great song of praise because movement is the first thing in creation.'

Roger T came to dance quite late, at the age of twenty-one. He studied at the Rambert for a while, then left for a number of independent teachers, such as Lydia Kyasht, Idzikovsky and Kathleen Crofton with whom he stayed for ten years. He danced in musical shows, joined a ballet company and toured various parts of the world.

'I started off being interested in choreography, but one was always having to change things because dancers couldn't or wouldn't do it. That's what drew me to teaching. I felt that the instruments, the dancers, had been trained so inadequately you couldn't get to the core of it. A whole generation of dancers had to be trained.'

It was while Roger T was working with Kathleen Crofton that he expressed his desire to teach, but nothing happened for two years until, one day, she suggested that he took the class. 'She explained to me later that what she had been waiting for was that one no longer taught from oneself, but was teaching from the tradition. Therefore, she said, you don't pass on your faults. Not that you haven't got them any more, but you're that much further behind them.'

Roger T teaches in a large studio behind the family house. He began with professional classes and he still teaches, every day of the week, a nucleus of professional dancers; there are also those who, having been taught by him in the past, come and work with him again. A number of Japanese dancers attend, as do sixty to seventy children, mainly on Saturdays but also after school. He starts them at the age of four and a half, 'for the very simple reason that they've got very few ideas about movement that are not their own. One approaches it from the point of view that there is a dancer in everybody. So I start with running and moving and skipping and responses to music. It's not until they are about seven or eight that one begins to teach them some of the forms of the classical dance.'

These classes are primarily for the one or two who may turn out to be professional dancers, but they seem to be valuable for the others also – they learn music, movement and a basic discipline – and numbers hold up. Originally, Roger T infiltrated the children into a beginner's class for adults. This worked surprisingly well for a time, the children bringing naturalness and the adults contributing concentration and stability. Then so many children started to arrive that the separate class was formed.

Roger T returns to what he sees as central to the dance, the classical tradition. 'That which is classical is that which is based on natural law and it is the natural law which holds the art. Across that you get laid fashion and all sorts of systems. The obvious law in relation to dance is the law of gravity. The dancer has to be centred or, one, he falls over and, two, he doesn't bring rest to the audience. With both the professionals and the children one tries to focus on this natural rising of movement and its channelling. There are two aspects to it: the movement and the form. It's like water, if it is to be of any use it must be put into cups and canals and things, otherwise it spills over. Really I feel more alive now as a teacher than I did as a performer, though I loved performing – but I have realized much more in the passing on of it.'

Full-time
Capital: studio at back of house
£1.50/£2.00 an hour for pianist
Income: £19 a twelve-week term/one hour Saturday morning/per child ('I put it up as I need more money')
professionals usually pay by the class: £1.50 for an hour and a half
Formal qualifications: none
Experience: dancing professionally

iii. English

1976: The English language has never been so popular; for various reasons everybody wants to learn it and many people come to England to do so. The language schools are very busy.

Elizabeth R, however, teaches English at home. Most of her students are foreigners: businessmen, diplomats, students and children. Other children, with learning or emotional difficulties, are sent from a local school for individual tuition. Elizabeth R is well versed for such a task. Head of the remedial section of a school, and later equipped with a teaching qualification from the International Language Centre, she found herself at home with two young children and spare time. She approached a nearby language school which recommended her to students. That was eight years ago and, apart from an attempt to teach in a comprehensive school, Elizabeth R has taught at home ever since. That is the way she prefers it: adults in the morning, children in the afternoon, the occasional outside visit to a family in the evening – on average, twenty hours a week, an hour at a time, except during the school holidays. The number of hours swing up and down, nothing constant about it, but it suits her other commitments of running a home and looking after a family. Occasionally something goes wrong, however. 'The children were ill in bed one day,' she recalls. 'I had one student who was late and the builder tramping round at the same time. Another potential student came to see me to arrange times and the next student turned up early. The final flourish was one of the children getting up and being sick down the stairs.' Now that the family has moved to a new house, one room is set aside for teaching, complete with books, tape-recorder, table and a seal of seclusion.

Students want all sorts of things from English but, principally, they want to understand and speak it. Elizabeth R teaches conversational English with basic grammar; another local freelance teacher takes those who want more formal work. It is the stimulus of so many different students which appeals to Elizabeth R; that and the necessity of constantly looking afresh at English and its meanings. Over cups of coffee students progress through the present, the continuous present, the interrogative and the negative, and are encouraged to talk from the start. No difficulty so far. The difficulty, or at any rate the part which is unusual, is the method of payment. Elizabeth R says, 'I don't want to know about money, I don't want to have anything to do with it. When people say, "How much do you charge?" I never say a flat fee. I always say, "How much do you think I'm worth?" which puts it back to them.' This method of settling fees has some interesting results. Some Iron Curtain nationals pay generously without further discussion; middle-class people round her way 'always insist on getting as much for their money as they can and the richer they are the less they pay. They always take ages to pay too.'

Ruby P is a teacher; she has taught part-time in the village primary school for over twenty years, ever since her youngest child was five. At that time schools were glad of part-time teachers, but at the moment even full-time teachers are being dismissed and there are certainly few jobs for part-time ones. There is another aspect to this picture of outsize classes and educational gloom: many parents are concerned about whether their children are being taught at all. Some are, some are probably not. Ruby P did a few weeks' supply teaching at a local school; then, when she left, she was asked to tutor her hairdresser's son, aged ten, who had got on so well with his new, albeit temporary, teacher. So for one hour on Saturday mornings Jonathan comes for his English lesson. It is a new experience for both of them. 'He's a nice, chatty little boy,' she says, 'not all that bright and not making much headway in his class, probably a bit lost in his big school. We do English, not maths at all because his maths is quite good and unless you're working with the teacher you can do more harm than good. It's his English which needs work. We cover basic grammar and we're reading a book and doing a lot of work with a junior dictionary.' Jonathan also has homework to do before his weekly lesson.

ELIZABETH R
Part-time (term-time)

Capital: none
  tape-recorder useful
  no separate premises
Income: A
Formal qualifications: from International Language Centre
Experience: teaching employment

RUBY P
Part-time
Capital: none
  no separate premises
Income: A
Formal qualifications: from Homerton teacher-training college
Experience: teaching employment

1980: Elizabeth R had to go into hospital and so gave up work. Ruby P now teaches the infants' class part-time in a local primary school.

CHAPTER SIX

Crafts & Manufactures

POTTERY

1976: Helen Y thinks it important to remember to 'see your craft in its historical context, not just for people of your generation and taste but to make use of anything which keeps the horizons wide and shows that you are not just this little person working away in a small workshop but part of a very big tradition'. For her, day-to-day pottery is domestic stoneware – plates, bowls, jugs, teapots, beakers – which she makes, fires and sells from her mews workshop. The workshop was chosen carefully, an inexpensive location near a well-heeled area, and bought on a nineteen-year lease with a legacy.

Before she gave up her job, Helen Y was a hobby potter. After a full-time two-year training course, and with a workshop newly equipped with kiln and extensive shelving and stocked with materials, she set to and finds that 'I can still say the same things about the work after ten years as I could after six months. It's rather more than half on commission and it's very local. The orders come from neighbours and friends. At the same time I can say that the pottery made here has gone to every continent, bought by people walking by.' All the pots are sold from the workshop; for Helen Y this is the best and simplest way. 'There has never been a time when there has been nothing in the books,' she says. 'Or, if the orders are a bit thin, there are gaps in the shelves, the casseroles are out of stock or the teapots are out of stock.' She works from one order to the next. If friends ask, 'How long are you going to go on doing this?' she answers, 'Well, I've got orders for the next three weeks,' and so it continues.

How does she manage to work so consistently from year to year without restlessness or boredom? 'I think you have to work very directly towards the order that has been given you,' she says, 'and try to see, in a subtle way, what it is that the customer is hoping to get. We all feel, when we are working, that we want to do something more individual, but that has to work in conjunction with the commission. If you just work on steadily and keep that customer in mind that really helps through this situation of working on your own. I find work is much sweetened in the context of the person who is either going to buy or use the thing that you are making. It makes the work easier to know that standards are important, because if you lose interest in it yourself that's when the work becomes heavy.'

Regular working hours, says Helen Y, help her; more difficult to maintain when on one's own, but necessary. 'You have to be rather cunning, use any subterfuge to avoid bouts of depression, go out for a walk for quarter of an hour, listen to the radio or television for a bit, have lunch with a friend – and then come back again. It's a combination of being disciplined and keeping at it and yet being resourceful and willing to do something different.'

A work book helps to keep life orderly. She has the one book, fourteen inches by nine inches with spongeable hard covers. Orders are written at the back. Work is written in detail at the front and made up into one unit, i.e. the filling of the kiln which is about two to three weeks' work. Notes about the firing of the kiln go in the same book and 'it is useful to keep these notes,' she says, 'particularly of glazes, recipes and the weights used in, for example, a set of teacups. Really it saves so much time in the end. Today I had to measure out enough clay to do eight plates of medium size. I got it out of the bin, weighed it up and there was literally no clay left over. It was exactly right.'

There is demand for her pots throughout the year, which increases at Christmas, slackens off in the New Year and picks up again at Easter. Helen Y has advertised in the past: in the borough guide, a handout at the cinema and, at Christmas, in the local newspaper. Now she relies only on her business card because 'people like to have something to show where the pot was made'.

Full-time
Capital: £8,000 bought lease of workshop with flat above and basic equipment
electric kiln was £300
'Don't be put off by these figures,' says Helen Y. 'You can build a kiln with bricks and, if you work hard, build up your business step by step with almost no capital at all.'
Income: A
Formal qualifications: from Harrow Art School

1980: 'I'm still working the same way.'

Full-time
Income: B

KNITTING

1976: Knitting has such a homely, plump image that it is not easy to remember what a robust yet delicate craft it is. Barbara A chanced on knitting almost as a joke. After mending Middle Eastern carpets for a year, she knitted a sleeping-bag for a baby which was intended to look like a carpet in pattern and colours. It worked; everybody was delighted.

Barbara A carried on mending carpets; then she bought a knitting machine for £100. 'The worst that can happen', she thought, 'is that I make some nice clothes for myself and the best that can happen is that I also make my money back.' She started to knit V-neck sweaters, scarves and hats, all to her own carpet designs. Then a year ago, friends opened a clothes shop and asked her to supply it; knitting output has since trebled and Barbara A now employs five knitters and two people who sew-up. She does all the designing on computer punch cards which fit into the machines and control the pattern, colour changes and so on. Her out-workers are paid by the piece; it works out at about £1 an hour. She estimates the wholesale price this way: 'I start with how long the garment is going to take,' she says. 'Is it a big job, is it complicated, therefore relative to everything else how much should I pay? Then I weigh it and find out how much wool there is and find out how complicated the sewing-up is. Then I add on a percentage for myself and that is the wholesale price.' She knits very little now. 'You get spoilt,' she says, 'a bit lazy, just scribbling away patterns, but I wouldn't want to knit three cardigans in a row anyway.'

Besides designing and occasionally knitting, Barbara A's job is to supply her out-workers with everything they need. 'I have a driver,' she says, 'who goes around.' It sounds very organized. 'Ye-es,' she says, 'it can sound that way, but downstairs there are two little bags which have to be delivered. There's two ounces of oatmeal wool that I have to send to one of my knitters because she's run out and the other one is ten ounces of willow and two ounces of something else and a punch card that I didn't have finished before.' Wool supplies are a problem. 'What I need is very difficult to find in the colours I want,' she says, 'because you might find the right weight and it will be bright red, bright pink or baby pink, white and black and school brown. The English colours are incredibly unimaginative. Wool is supposed to be traditional to England; it just isn't, there are a lot of synthetics.' After searching she found wool in the colours and quantities she wanted in Scotland and France.

The shop helps a good deal in feeding back information of the 'sleeves are too short' kind. 'I spend a lot of time at the shop,' says Barbara A. 'This week I'm going to be there every day because someone wants to be measured for something, someone wants to discuss a new colour scheme or what would match a skirt they've bought.' Self-employed people sometimes prefer working on their own; Barbara A prefers company. 'I was going out of my mind through lack of stimulation when I was carpet mending,' she says. The shop provides a better balance.

Barbara A's approach would not suit everybody, because every knitter has a different way of working and a different market. Her clothes come under 'what is labelled the ethnic look,' she says, 'though I think I can survive after the ethnic look is over. I'm going to move away from it before it moves away from me; they know what sells in the shop and we're going to get some new designs together.' She admits to lots of mistakes. 'When the shop opened it was February and the fashion magazines say that people are buying for summer. So we threw together a summer collection which was a bit of a flop, but the winter stuff went right on selling.'

Although she has been knitting since she was eight, Barbara A never treated it seriously. Her art-school training did nothing to teach her otherwise. 'The American system of education is great for teaching people to dabble,' she says, 'and it convinced me that knitting was mundane and should be avoided at all costs, whereas it was obvious that was where I needed to go.' Coming to England on a working holiday she decided to stay, and the easiest way to stay was to be self-employed. As a matter of fact she started up a company, far too soon and probably unnecessary, she says, but 'it was interesting, it took on a personality of its own. I suddenly had to make a go of it, I had to do justice to this separate entity.'

Eight months later: 'I've started exporting,' says Barbara A. 'I've got two clients in Germany. One of them came to the shop and asked me to supply her shop in Munich and the other one came to a show which friends were having. It's now about half my business. While not much has been sold in the shop over the summer I've been able to get on and supply new clients. Exporting is not that difficult, it's done through an air shippers. I have to be a bit more careful with the invoices, get proof of VAT, that sort of thing.'

Full-time
Capital: £100 for knitting machine
  out-workers £1 an hour
  driver £10 for around fifty miles
  no separate premises
Income: A/B
Formal qualifications: from art school

1980: Barbara A met Brendan, got married and is now expecting a baby.

'I have not gone off knitting or designing, but I have gone off developing a business. When the wolf is no longer at the door you lose the impetus and there is a different reason for working. When I was running the business at full blast I didn't do anything else. I would be on a bus and all I saw were people's sweaters. When something else came along, that was fulfilling, I let the business get smaller and stopped looking for work.

'What I longed for was to design for love not money – that was my real goal in life. I wanted to improve the quality and make the work more personalized, so I spent long hours at the knitting machine. But then I ran out of steam design-wise and in the spring of '79 Brendan reminded me that, if I was going to get the new designs ready for that season, I had to do it now. I had to make a decision one way or the other. Someone offered me a job and that was a wonderful excuse, since I really wanted to be pregnant. Now I just love doing up the house . . . spending an enormous amount of time on making a cover for the headboard for the bed.'

There was another reason why Barbara was able to give up the business when she did. 'When I got married my status with the Home Office changed and I got permanent residence in this country. Before that I had a yearly visa and I got permission to form a limited company and this was stamped in my passport. The visa was given to me provided I did not take a job or change my employment without the permission of the Secretary of State. If I had done so, I would have had trouble getting my visa renewed. And of course I couldn't take a job because I was supposed to be offering work to people instead of taking work that a UK national could do. Now all that has changed – but that was one reason why I had to persevere with the business.'

SADDLERY

1976: 'What started me', says Paul D, 'was that I hadn't found a saddle I was comfortable on. I thought I would make a comfortable saddle. I did but I ended up selling it.' That was in the Camargue two years ago, while staying with his father, where there wasn't much else to do. A little previous experience in saddle repairs and skills in wood – cabinet making, antique restoration, instrument repairs – and in making leather handbags all contributed towards creating a saddle, but 'it's a matter of commonsense,' says Paul D. 'You take something apart and you can see how it is made. If you're observant you look at what you're doing and it's not so complicated. You can put something on a horse and see where it isn't fitting. It's like a shoe. There are certain tricks, obviously, as there are in anything. You have to know something about anatomy otherwise you can do a horse awful damage. You just learn by practising and talking to people.'

Paul D is currently working on two types of saddle: one for disabled people and another, similar, for trekking. The saddles are still at the prototype stage. He has chosen a specialized field. 'The only way I can make a living', he says, 'is to do something which nobody else is doing.' It makes sense in an area where most standard English saddles come from Walsall and others are imported from such countries as Switzerland, Italy and the Argentine. There are a few craftsmen working on made-to-order saddles, especially racing saddles, but the trees (the wooden base) are nowadays bought from wholesalers. Paul D makes his. 'In any case, Western saddles [which he also makes] can't be mass-produced. You have to make the tree and mould the leather before it is cut.' There are outlets, he says, which need developing. Film work is one. 'In films of jousting, for example, I've often seen them doing it on ordinary English saddles and that's not how it should be.'

Both his saddles for the disabled and the trekking saddles have been designed to clip together for ease of repair and should work well in theory – in theory because they have yet to be sold and commercially tested. There are various organizations which might be interested. 'All I can do is get the saddles photographed, make up a brochure and send it to them,' he says. At the rate of around two a week, or more if he works hard on several at a time, the saddles will retail at about £80, of which about £25 will be materials. It took some time initially to develop the patterns and moulds and at least one manufacturer has shown an interest in buying the patterns, but 'I'd be cutting my throat because I need an income,' he says. 'It's the ideal work for me; it's very relaxing and I'm quite a slow worker because I'm fairly meticulous.'

While the saddlery is getting going, Paul D is working on other things: a bit of shop furnishing, a bit of sculpture. 'I'm quite multifaceted,' he admits, 'and it's very awkward; you're going in all directions at once. Eventually I want to live on saddlery, but even then I shall be doing other things, simply because I get bored with any one thing. Being self-employed, it's really difficult to discipline yourself. I probably work as long hours as anybody but it's all spread around.' Another problem for him is organizing the selling side. He puts it this way: 'I make something and once it's finished I'm not interested in it any more, it's served its purpose. I'd as soon give it away, which isn't very good business.' In France there was a buyer for every saddle he made before it was finished; he doesn't yet know about England.

Nine months later: 'I've moved to Hampshire and I'm converting a barn into a workshop there. The trekking saddles are being sold to a trekking centre in the Camargue and a shop in Paris. The Riding for the Disabled Association in this country has no money to spare for the other type of saddle, but it has been taken up as a dressage saddle by a Spaniard breaking horses – again in the Camargue. French customs charge forty per cent duty on imported saddles but, even so, there seems to be a demand for them. I'm still under-capitalized and waiting for money from France so I can stock up on materials.'

Part-time
Capital: materials – saddle £25, Western saddle £90
  workshop
Income: A/B
Formal qualifications: none
Experience: in wood, leather, sculpture, shop furnishing

CLOCK CASES

1980: Paul D has left saddlery (above) to construct grandfather-clock cases. While making dressage saddles for export to France, he went to work for an antique restorer to earn some money. A 1685 Dutch clock case came in, which he repaired for £450; thereafter, Paul D was given all the clock-case repair work.

That was two or three years ago and Paul D has been making clock cases ever since, for collectors and for people who find themselves in possession of a rotted case – or no case at all. He has researched into makers and districts and, from this data, discovers the date of the movement. A plain oak case could take a week to make, an elaborate case three or four weeks, and he has made thirty so far.

In Farnham, where he now lives, Paul D met an horologist and made cases for him. The horologist had good contacts and Paul's work prospered. 'This is the longest I've stuck at anything. I do it to earn a living and because there is a demand for it and because I'm good at it. And I'm self-employed and can suit myself. Really, I would like to be a sculptor, but I don't think I will make any money at that! I have to turn this business into a successful one, especially now that I'm married.'

Being successful in this sense means getting the money side well organized, which means getting orders and getting paid. Paul D is acutely aware of the problems of marketing – his saddles were so slow to sell – but he is helped by a renewed public interest in clocks. Last year, at an exhibition at the Commonwealth Institute attended by 2,000 people, Paul D met a clock maker (he who fashions the movements) and the two of them are producing a limited edition of six to ten grandfather clocks which will sell at £2,900 each. The movement, he says, will be identical to one of 1690 and the case will be of the same period. They intend to put a colour advertisement in *Clocks* magazine and expect to sell the lot.

Paul D normally gets paid, but not necessarily on time. It is capital, as always with small businesses, that is the problem. 'When you start any business there are lots of debts and when I first moved to Farnham I was paying £60 a month rent, £80 a month for the car and £70 a month for the workshop – and there was no money coming in.

'I very badly needed capital but it seemed impossible to get. I went from the bank to the Citizens Advice Bureau to CoSIRA, who said they couldn't help because I wasn't in a rural area. In the end my father-in-law underwrote an overdraft at the bank. I had to buy a lot of tools and pay my debts and even now I find myself held up because I can't buy the wood to make the cases. But it is beginning to work out. I have £2,500 worth of orders and I've just bought a load of timber for five cases costing £1,500. Now I ask a quarter deposit from clients before starting work.'

Full-time
Capital: overdraft at bank
  no separate premises
Income: D ('if I got paid on time')

LEATHER

1976: For Gary D, an Australian surfer and factory worker, leather work started in 1969 with an invitation from an American on the Queensland Gold Coast to 'come down here and help me out. I'll show you what to do, show you a way of living.' It was no apprenticeship that first year, but he learnt enough of the basic laws of working with leather ('what to do and what not to do') and techniques of buying hides and selling the finished bags to bring him over to England.

In London, Gary D worked for six months with a leather company classifying and grading leather; then he took off for California and St Augustine in Florida. The American tradition of leather work is rich in techniques, styles and patterns and while he was making belts, watchbands, bags, hair-slides and wallets Gary D was also refining and developing his work. On one occasion, he recalls, he was told that '"the belts are just great, but the rivets, you're not doing those properly, it spoils the whole thing". You do the whole belt perfectly and you come to the last part, just two little rivets and you mess those up, do one a little bit crooked, little things like that you remember, it makes the whole difference.'

Virtually all his work is for a tourist market and, back in England, he went down to Cornwall where he set up with a sandal maker in Newquay. 'It was very basic leather work,' says Gary D, 'no tooling or fancy work on the outside. They had leather uppers and tire soles and they were selling all right because they were long-wearing.' This arrangement went on for three years, Gary D introducing new work and new ideas. He would go down and 'work my butt off in the summer and in the winter you had enough money to last you, if you were lucky, to come back and set up the next summer'. Tourist work is usually seasonal and it suited Gary D; he would winter in Morocco, India and Ceylon – intensive spells of work seasoned with intensive spells of lotus living.

However, it couldn't last. The Newquay sandal maker took all his ideas and is now mass-producing; Gary D moved back to London, got married and asked a leather-worker friend in Australia to be his partner. 'London is the largest tourist attraction in the world,' he wrote. 'The economy isn't too good, but if you come over we'll get something going.' It was the summer of 1975 and they worked outside in the garden well into the evening; but that couldn't last and the search for a workshop began in earnest as the days got colder. Finding a workshop at the right price can be a tedious operation for urban craftsmen, but eventually Gary D and partner were offered space at Camden Lock rented from a silversmith. It costs them £3 a week each. This is how things stand at the moment, and they work throughout the week to produce enough for the weekend markets (see page 50). Their output is mainly belts since 'we've found these to be the most popular, the easiest to make and the fastest to make because we make everything by hand'. Despite a sour economic climate, their work has been selling well. Leather work used to be one of those crafts which flooded the market with badly made goods; not any longer, says Gary D. 'A lot of leather workers have quit, their work wasn't very good. After six years I know how to finish it off properly, which is where a lot of people fail. The cost of leather is going up and it is only those people who are doing a little bit extra who will survive.' Gary D has found his market and prices his goods carefully. 'People have a set amount of pounds they want to spend, that's about £3 or £4. So we keep ourselves in that bracket.'

During the day, Gary D works as a cashier for an advertising agency. The job serves a double purpose: it will enable him to get a mortgage for a flat he and his wife are buying and it gives him a practical insight into how a small business is run. An evening class in accountancy and book-keeping tops up that side of things.

Eight months later: 'I've been working full-time at the workshops since April, given up the job, and it's going pretty well; going up and down a lot, I only made 31p last week! On another week I might make £200. We've given up Portobello Road but we still go to Petticoat Lane and another market in the city, St Christopher's Place, three times a week. Belts are still our main line, but we make anything useful in leather: bags, passport pouches, wristbands and custom-made sandals. We're really working seven days a week.'

Full-time
Capital: rent of workshop £30 a month (new rates)
tools worth about £800 between the two partners
Income: B
Formal qualifications: none

1980: Gary D was in England for a few months before going back to Australia where he had spent a year working as a storeman for a shoe manufacturer, making stained-glass windows and boxes and buying a twelve-acre plot in Queensland. When he returns he will build a house on his land, grow cut flowers, nuts and avocados and work with stained glass.

Not leather? 'No, I felt like a change, I had been working with leather for eight years. The cost of leather quadrupled in a couple of months, the public couldn't take the leap in prices, so you had to stick to bread-and-butter work because that paid the money – unless you're in Bond Street where your clientele is different and you can afford to do one-off jobs.'

Learning about stained glass when he was working in America and at Camden Lock, Gary D discovered that in Australia 'it is like starting leatherwork fifteen years ago, you have to educate people about stained glass. Church windows are the only thing they can compare it with. Stained glass is also very expensive and one of my reasons for coming to England was to find suppliers of glass so I can import it.' He is returning to Australia equipped with lists of suppliers and useful addresses. He is also returning with building experience: carpentry and brick-laying, skills which he previously had, but which he has developed working as a builder in London. 'I haven't advertised, I've just got jobs through word-of-mouth; it's about the only business where you can make reasonable money quickly. I only charge £3 an hour but regular builders work for £5 or £6. I do a good job, that was one of the reasons I did it; I take a little longer but in the end it turns out a bit cheaper for the client.

'My partner in the leather business did a TOPS course in carpentry and he's now a fully fledged carpenter, self-employed. He put one ad. in the *Hackney Gazette* and got three months' work out of the one advertisement.'

While in London, Gary D has taken evening classes in brick-laying and plumbing, 'so I can build a house from scratch' on the Queensland plot. 'When I was on the land I felt inspired, I felt really fit and enthusiastic and I learnt things every day by watching the animals and bugs and birds and plants – everything fell into place. It's isolated but only twelve miles from big towns. It's something I always wanted to do, to live close to the land.'

CLOTHES DESIGN

1976: John D and his wife Molly work tucked into a prefab workshop away from the main commercial world, so 'we only see those people who really want to see us,' they say. They make silk-screened clothes: waistcoats, jackets, t-shirts, 'celebrating in print the things we come across', whether it's fat strawberries, neon lights, tattoos or exploding martinis. Molly D's mother makes up the t-shirts and other friends help with sewing up the clothes, which are sold to manufacturers and fashion houses all over the world. Not everybody wants, or can afford, their clothes, but those who do are enthusiasts. Selling is the least of their problems; not that they have so many problems, their work is in great demand, but as John D says, 'If you create a demand it's your responsibility to supply it,' and that sometimes means a seven-day week.

Their problem is how to stay small and steady. In their three or four years of full-time silk-screening they have received special offers from the *Sunday Times* and several companies coming to them with massive orders. 'Avoid it like the plague,' says John D. 'It means getting a huge overdraft, employing lots of people; avoid getting too big.' Then there are those who would like to buy them up and 'that's very dangerous,' adds Molly D. 'Those sort of people collect people, use them up and throw them away. That's one thing we've always steered clear of.'

Leaving art school with fine art and textile experience, they both taught and Molly D did a few prints and clothes while John D painted, sculpted and did illustration work. Then, five years ago, they landed a workshop space with other artists and craftsmen and started work there. 'It was the first time we had a chance to set up a print table,' says John D. 'Before that we had a big dining table and a couple of blankets. We started printing things we had ideas for, peddled them around and sold them.' After a while offers started coming in so they dropped their other work and concentrated on printing 'because that's the one that took off'. Molly D designs the clothes and they both design the prints; they run them for as long as there is a demand, perhaps two thousand finished articles or twelve thousand. Molly also has the children to care for; the two eldest go to school and she brings the youngest to the workshop. They are buying a maisonette at the back at the workshop to make home/work organization easier.

The workshop itself is run as a co-operative trust; however, about half the artists/craftsmen rarely use it and this 'has affected the work of other people', says John D. 'Anybody who wanted the space could have it, which was a mistake because there are a lot of people for whom it has been a pipe dream. It takes weeks to arrange a meeting and then you never get a total decision.' This run-down is going to be halted, they say; apart from anything else they are applying for a new lease from the council, so everything must be thriving and vigorous.

John and Molly D intend to go on as before, perhaps taking up work in the States, perhaps making a film, perhaps not. 'It's all circumstantial,' says John D; 'when the circumstances are right, you do something, right?' He is sceptical about an approach which says, in advance, 'I have decided to do this or that and I am going to earn a living from it.' The 'what can I do?' attitude, he says, does not work. 'Let's put it this way. If you want to go into silk-screening as a livelihood, choose something else. But if you want to get into it because you're interested in print and you just want to experiment and then, later, if you're lucky . . . that sort of approach, yes. Start on the kitchen table, it's easy. It only costs £30 to get the equipment together. I do think if you can find a way of working on your own, go out of your way to do it; it's much better even if you fail.' John D says that he couldn't give advice. 'I would say, "Don't give advice, go your own way." I'd give practical help but you can't give advice, everyone's lifeline is different.' For the two of them success is 'getting your life together to make your life work for you' and 'anyway you can't tell when you've got it'.

Eight months later: The workshop has been reorganized, the maisonette is bought, but 'we didn't go to the States,' says John D. 'For the last five months things have been really happening and all my little plans for getting out of the doldrums, like going to the States, I've just left those. We're bringing in a new table and designing quilts, bed quilts. The first one will commemorate the first British Beatles Convention and then we'll see.'

Full-time
Capital: for a beginner £30 to £40 covers basic equipment
separate working premises
out-workers paid by piece according to skill and complexity of garment
Income: C (each)
Formal qualifications: from art school (John D in fine art; Molly D in textiles)

1980: John and Molly D continue to print and make clothes in the workshop. The reason for staying small, they say, is that you can change easily, whereas if you want to do something as a lifelong business you expand. But you can't be open-ended with a large-scale set-up. During the last five years they have turned towards punk culture; the clothes they make reflect this as do the clothes they wear. Out went the multi-coloured knits and in came leather. This year they will be making clothes from 'junk': old fabrics, clothes, boots, bags, 'anything that will make a garment that's warm, comfortable and still attractive. The whole idea of fashion is a built-in obsolescence. It forces people to change more than they need to in their dress. Why do people need seven or eight suits, five pairs of boots, seven pairs of shoes? They don't.'

All the clothes, except the jeans, are made in one small room, while the larger room is used for screen-printing. The jeans are made in a factory 'because it's the only practical way to make a pair of trousers – there are about eight different machines involved in the manufacture of trousers'. The clothes sell easily because, as John D says, 'it's the fact that they're different, people will go out of their way to get them. Our prices aren't that great, you can get a cheaper pair of trousers, a cheaper T-shirt. But we do what nobody else does, it's as simple as that.'

Full-time
Income: D

BABY SLINGS

1979: When Yolande H left her job with a health-food restaurant to have a baby she turned her attention to making baby clothes and buying nursery equipment. She didn't want a pram, convinced that a sling is the most natural and comforting way for parent and child to be together. When Anna was born, the sling she had bought did not give the proper head support and it was also difficult to use. So Yolande started to think of ways of improving the design.

Even before the baby was born she and her husband, George, a leather-worker who had a job with the mentally handicapped, had decided to work from home in Northampton and set up a business together, 'but we didn't know what our product was going to be. We went a whole year ripe for something to happen. We were ready, when Anna was born, and we saw the need for a baby sling. It was just like dropping a seed into a very fertile seed bed.'

Design, says Yolande H, is all commonsense. 'When you sit down to design something you decide what you need, write long lists of what you need and how to apply it. We made five prototypes, changing a bit here, a bit there. There was a very expensive American sling on the market but it was so cumbersome. As soon as we saw there was a need for something that wasn't being supplied on the market, we just went about doing it. It's been amazing the amount of help we've had . . . Whenever we've needed something, somebody has walked in and known everything about it.'

The first one hundred slings were made from a hundred metres of denim by Yolande with shears and the sewing machine on the bedroom floor. They sold out in three weeks after an advertisement and article in *Time Out*. They invested in another two rolls of denim and, since Yolande had had enough of the bedroom floor, looked for workshop space and equipment.

At that point assistance appeared in the shape of a manufacturer for Marks & Spencer, who gave good advice on the production side and sold them a second-hand twenty foot by five foot cutting table, with a big roll-holder at one end and an electric material cutter to cut up to one hundred layers of material in one slice. Another friend contributed by designing the advertisements and leaflet artwork. A retired cost accountant helped on the accountancy and marketing side and analysed the costing to produce competitive prices. George and Yolande H very quickly found a 560-square-foot workshop – albeit in a dilapidated condition – at a low rent from an art restorer, who happened to be interested in encouraging small businesses.

George and Yolande H do the cutting and marketing and two local mothers do all the sewing. They sell about thirty to forty slings a week. George H left his job: 'We spend most of our time doing office work now,' he says. 'It's very strange to us, because we're very practical people used to making things, but we have to convince ourselves that we're working when we're sitting down and scratching our heads and thinking about advertising. I'm the factory boy and the packer still. Sales would have to go up five times before we could think of employing somebody to do the cutting and packing and out-worker deliveries.' George's job had of course paid the mortgage and the bills. When he left they were on their own financially.

What George and Yolande H aim to produce is an article that 'hasn't been skimped on quality but can also be sold profitably and competitively'. Costing is the key to success here. 'The prime costing (materials and labour) comes to about £4 a sling. Overheads on top of that are relative to the production and you can't talk about a realistic costing unless you relate it to a production figure and on the production figure we are hoping to reach – fifty a week – the price we are selling it at would be quite realistic, but restrictive if we wanted to move into a mass market. If we wanted to go into the retail market, rather than rely on mail order, we might have to cut prices, but we *must* know what it's costing us.'

The slings are currently sold entirely by mail order through advertisements in *Mother & Baby*, *Mother*, *Parents* and the quality Sunday newspapers. 'We have to watch advertising,' says George H, 'because it can get very expensive, especially in the initial stages when it's much more of a gamble. The time when you place your ads can count for quite a lot; slings are rather a summery thing. Also our market is for the first-born baby so *Mother* magazine is a bit old for us, they go for the mothers who already have children.'

George and Yolande H have been approached by a company in Yorkshire to sell their baby slings on the retail market. They are considering the offer but would retain the mail order, 'otherwise, if we put all our eggs in one basket, there is a danger of them taking us over'.

Even if they supplied a larger company, the sling would still find its place at the top end of the market because 'we don't produce a cheap sling. We shouldn't have competition because the market isn't big enough for the people who mass produce to come in.' The price has to be right, 'not with such a big margin that people can take the design and produce it more cheaply. In fact, we have registered the design – but not against a shark who puts a button in a different place . . . The best protection is the best article at the most competitive price.'

When it comes down to it, they must sell to survive but the sling has to be the best. It was, after all, intended for their daughter, Anna. 'The essence of the sling is that it should be the very best quality materials and design. For the father or mother whose child is in there, they're carrying the most valuable, precious thing they've got. So quality right the way through, not just in the material you can see but also the foam that goes inside and the thread that we bought to stitch it together.'

With eight months of business behind them, George and Yolande H are looking to their next product, probably a foldaway baby bed, 'so that, when the sling is reaching its peak, we've got something else coming along. If it's all going well and you think "fantastic", it's like harvesting all your grain without thinking about what's going to happen next year. You've got all the time to be planting new seeds as well as harvesting. It's like what's happening in today's industry, we're harvesting what's happened fifty, a hundred years ago. You must be planting fresh all the time.

'The essential ingredients for going self-employed,' says Yolande H, 'are not how much money you have but what sort of opening you have got in the market – and somehow it magically appears, you sell it and make money. It starts with the people themselves. We were ripe for some enterprise a year before it happened and we'd had a lot of experience. We have no qualifications – but we have all the qualifications in the world because we've done lots of practical work, we know how to apply ourselves. When you see a problem you have a lot of resources within yourself. How do you design something? How do you set about doing it? You think about it, apply yourself and you find that you wash yourself in it, you come up with things, it just happens naturally.'

Full-time (they both look after Anna)
Capital: £300 for cutting table plus electric cutter (second-hand)
  £200 on doing up workshop
  car essential for out-worker deliveries
  out-workers £1 an hour basic (they make two to two-and-a-half times as much)
Income: basic sling £10.99
  deluxe sling £12.99
  showerproof overall £1.99
Formal qualifications: none
Experience: a variety of work between them

1981: Yolande and George H have not had an easy time during the last year. There were personal and other unforeseen problems which complicated their working life. One of their main difficulties has been the high cost of advertising. The baby slings were selling but the advertising was eating into their profit margin. Deciding to stop advertising they circulated baby clinics with leaflets, producing fewer sales but higher profits.

One thing led to another. Since there was no longer enough work to keep both of them occupied all week George H got an evening job and Yolande kept the business running, treating its earnings as a bonus. That is how the situation stands at the moment.

MAIL ORDER for clothes (see page 54).

MUSICAL INSTRUMENTS

1976: Michael S had a saw and a plane when he first started to make lutes. There was no money to spare from his factory work so he went to a demolition site and picked up enough wood for a bench. A bending iron – for bending the ribs of the lute – was made from an old electric fire which someone had thrown out. 'I didn't spend any money on equipment at all,' he says. 'I just improvised.'

The sound of Renaissance music – 'it has a still quality' – and the wish to have his own business came together in an instrument – the lute – and then, later, rebecs and baroque guitars. A sculptor by training, Michael S had very little experience with wood, but 'when I was younger I had the feeling that I could do anything I wanted to do if I put my mind to it and it seemed a relatively easy job to make a musical instrument'. Basically, he says, 'one has to be able to cut a straight line and plane a flat surface, to do some cutting with a knife, carefully, for example with the rose, understand something about volume and be able to visualize how things go together'. After seeing a lute at a concert for the first time, another lute maker introduced him to the techniques of making one from beginning to end. With an instrument in his hands, he drew it and constructed his own. Another lute followed, which found its way to Canada, and Michael S stopped work at the factory. It was 1971.

Anybody, so he says, can make a musical instrument of sorts; it is the sound which emerges from it which distinguishes one craftsman from another. 'It's the tensions and pitches which have evolved,' he says. 'I suppose I have quite a good ear for listening because that's all one needs to have. I don't even play a lute very well. It's the technicalities which one has to get over initially. You can't learn from books. The only thing to do is go ahead; the more you do it the more you understand it is like it is and what is needed.'

Musicians make a very discriminating market, found partly through advertising but mainly through reputation. Beginner makers sell mostly to beginner players and then a lute, moderately priced, would fetch around £250 to £300. Lutes sold abroad can be double the UK price. Most lute makers have a long waiting list. 'What happens', says Michael S, 'is that you start off with an order, then two orders, and then the waiting list is six months, then a year, then four years. Now while all those people are waiting for lutes, and are prepared to wait, there are other people eagerly trying to get hold of lutes, so they go to new makers who have a waiting list of two months.' So it continues. It takes about a month to make a lute 'with all the bits and pieces one has to do, buy materials, answer the phone and deal with Fred who wants to come round and talk about lutes for three hours'. Lots of people want to talk about lutes. Early music is on a revival and good instrument makers are in demand. It takes time, however, to develop the essential skills.

Michael S restored his workshop two and a half years ago with another lute maker who has since left. 'He couldn't keep going,' says Michael S, 'because he had three children and a wife to support. He started after I did but I feel that if he had carried on he might be all right now, but it wasn't secure enough at the time.'

The workshop is currently occupied by himself, another lute maker and, starting next week, a keyboard-instrument maker. They share the rent and some of the equipment. 'He uses my circular saw and I use his G-clamps every now and again,' says Michael S. Other tools, such as hole cutters and peg sharpeners, they make themselves. 'We make them all the time,' he says, 'use them for a while, they get worn out, so we make another.'

Nine months later: 'As more information on old lutes becomes available,' says Michael S, 'I'm finding that our discoveries are becoming an integral part of making new ones. It's a matter of refining details: woods, pegs, thicknesses, string tensions, spacing. There's also a new workshop opened next to the Music Centre and there are five extra people making musical instruments. It's really good to work with others; we pass on information and we've just bought our first load of wood together.'

Full-time
Capital: none at beginning
  tools cost £800 (including grindstone, bandsaw, circular saw and planer)
  cost of making one instrument £30 to £40 (soundboard £10, pegs £12 to £15, strings £8)
  instrument case costs £54
  rent of workshop £30 (shared between three)
Income: C
Formal qualifications: none
Experience: as sculptor

1980: In May 1979 Michael S went to southern California, from where he writes: 'So much has happened since I saw you last. Lute making progressed well for me. Until May '77 I was working on my own; then I was joined by an assistant who worked with me for about one and a half years which boosted production, but I was not any better off financially. To make a leap financially I discovered that I needed to employ more people, but found that so much time was spent organizing instead of making. I also worked with the Early Music Centre, helping to run it, and held a class in lute making on Monday evenings for two years.'

Wanting to research and explore new areas, Michael S went to the States with only a few suitcases and handtools. He also got married. 'A year has passed and I have been flitting from one thing to another to find out what the next step may be. I am now working with a new company which is producing stained-art glass and I am hand rolling it, learning how to make glass from sand, casting, blowing, leading and copper foiling. So I have a golden opportunity to move in any direction within glass that I wish. I have been making decorative stamps to press into the molten glass. It is a new and exciting area to work in for me and I feel I can enjoy making the occasional lute without it being an intense thing. Where this is going to lead I do not know, but it is exciting.'

According to the Early Music Centre, English lute prices have caught up with continental prices and range between £140 and £1,500. Good instruments start from £200. Lutes are sometimes being made on semi-industrial lines: twelve soundboards, two hundred pegs at a time, etc.

PICTURE FRAMING

1976: What can you do if you don't have a job and you can't speak the language too well? 'I didn't know what to do,' says Christian G. 'I had always wanted to work with my hands and one day a friend said, "Why not try picture framing?" I was hesitating between picture framing and book binding and I found the picture-framing work first.' Apprenticed to an old-established picture-framing firm for two-and-a-half years, Christian G learnt the fundamentals of his craft including gilding. He recommends an apprenticeship: 'You are always learning, especially in restoration. You can spend six months on a course and you know the rudiments, but you've got to work on different jobs over a period of time to know what to do.' He adds, 'I thought I was very clumsy before I started this work.'

Seven months ago he set up in partnership with the foreman of the firm. 'He is coming at night and on Saturdays,' says Christian G, 'and I hope that in six months or a year we will be able to work full-time together.' Work has been no problem. Perhaps they have been lucky. In any case, when a gallery asked them to supply frames for pictures in the World of Islam festival they were ready. A friend makes most of the frames and Christian G does the gilding. He charges £2.50 an hour and works, on average, about six hours a day. 'I am interested in the money,' he says, 'but it is not the main thing. To be able to work when I wanted to, two hours a day or even at night – that was the main thing.' It is too soon to say how the work will eventually stabilize. Christian G knows the direction in which he would like to go: 'Simple framing, especially classical or restoration framing,' he says. It is not only a craft in itself; the picture framer also needs to know about painting and a bit about furniture.

Besides gallery connections, many picture framers take in work from the general public. Gallery work, however, is better paid. 'I am not expensive,' says Christian G, 'but I am charging a fair price because I do more work than a normal picture framer.' His prices are still less than West End framers, largely because his overheads are much lower. 'The galleries go to these pictures framers,' he says, 'but the price is too high for them. That's how I get my deal.' Then, 'you have to have a competitive price. If you are too expensive you are not going to get work, especially if you have a small workshop and you have no name. To establish a picture-framing business you have to work from mouth to ear, it takes quite a long time.'

Christian G found it easy to start his workshop. In Paris, he says, it would have been much harder, much more expensive to find a place to work. In England, 'if you know your trade and have a bit of money on your side, you can start like that with no official permission, no permit'. He had no money at all, but borrowed £2,000 – more than enough – 'because I wasn't expecting work to come so quickly. I spent about £650 on buying equipment and £250 on key money.' A major outlay is £300 a month on gold leaf. 'I get it back, but I need that amount. If I didn't have the money,' he says, 'I would go to a gallery, because there are few people doing gilding apart from the established firms, and ask them to lend me some money while I was working for them. I am sure this kind of thing is possible.'

Six months later: 'I am working for two galleries,' says Christian G, 'the one I first mentioned and now another one. There is a lot of work and it is going very well, which is good because I have just bought a house.'

Full-time
Capital: £2,000
  equipment cost about £650
  rent of workshop £69 a month
Income: C
Formal qualifications: apprenticeship

1980: Christian G is moving to a light industrial area, to a workshop ten times the size of his present one. He will be joined by his partner who, after twenty-five years in an old-established firm, has finally left his job and will be working with him on restoring old frames and making reproduction ones. They will share a workshop and the workload, but remain sole traders.

There are not many skilled gilders around – certainly not self-employed ones – and Christian G has as much work as he can handle. He continues to supply West End galleries, making rich, gold frames to surround nineteenth-century paintings destined for the Emirates. He also enjoys restoring old frames and, for him, the art of restoration is a satisfying puzzle that the craftsman's knowledge can unlock. 'With each one it's a different approach, you have to find out the problem; it may have been restored before, or it may react badly to restoration . . . This one was a real mess before it was restored; it wasn't worth the money spent, but it suited the painting and it was the original frame and the bloke wanted it . . . But a frame like this is Queen Anne, beautiful frame, carved wood, it would be worth restoring even if it was a wreck. In fact, there's not much to do, a few chips and you have to change the colour of the gold, it's too bright.'

According to Christian G, the reason why there aren't many gilders is that the old craftsmen kept their secrets very closely guarded. 'If you go to the colleges, they'll teach you something which could be taught in two weeks. If you work in a workshop, you'll be able to lay the gold and burnish it and prepare the frame for finishing . . . I've been lucky because my partner knows the old skills. But he's never been taught. He got his knowledge by testing all the jars that were lying around.'

Full-time
Income: £5 + an hour
Christian G spends about £600 a month on gold

MODEL SHIPS

1976: Some people have hobbies; others, like Jonathan T, have model making. 'It grips you,' he says. At the age of seventeen he gave it up: 'I can remember it, a conscious decision that it was too private, too inward-looking.' Now, twenty years later, restoring and rigging model ships is half his livelihood. The other half is graphic design. Both activities are going well. In graphic design he has got to the point where he can choose the bigger jobs, but model ships are also on the increase, either battered hulks requiring a complete overhaul or sleek hulls needing a canopy of rigging. He will take any type of sailing ship: waiting in his workshop were a modern Greek yacht and a number of tiny wood-and-bone ships made by Napoleonic prisoners-of-war.

Model ship restoration took off for Jonathan T in 1967; the first was a ship in a bottle belonging to his parents-in-law and then others came in through the Parker Gallery. In addition, 'there was an old boy in Lancashire who used to make nice hulls, but he wasn't interested in masting and rigging, the string bit. I used to get these almost perfectly finished hulls and do all the masting and rigging.' The supply of beaten-up ships flows on. 'I've gone through the first phase one seems to go through,' he says, 'of (a) finding out what one can do and (b) living through one's dreams of what one wants to do. This slightly antiquey, craftsmanship type, I'm beginning to realize it more and more, that really is me. It's beginning to gel.'

Ship models are, of course, only one tributary of a whole stream of modelling. Jonathan T also makes chess figures. 'I've done a little work, and there is probably more if I could find it, replacing chess figures, little oriental pieces. They're generally carved in ivory. I replaced them in holly wood which is almost dead white and very, very hard.' Then there is heraldry: 'I painted a coat of arms on a coach just before Christmas.' Isn't that very specialized? 'You have to do a bit of research, but I've got a continuing interest in history,' he says.

Despite other interests, Jonathan T loves ships the best. 'The shape of the hull is so beautiful,' he says, 'It's total economy, a balance between wind and water, nothing superfluous except perhaps the scrolling round the figurehead.' He describes his approach to the work: 'It's highly technical and highly detailed. I sometimes feel akin to the dentist, I think we're in similar lines of business. The detail is just a certain sort of richness. It takes so long to do. You end up with a whole and the richness of the whole is due to the fact that it's full, it's completely composed. There are countless little bits and pieces which, though they're pretty unimportant in themselves, they're so small, you've put in maximum effort to every little piece and it builds up. The total is greater than the sum of its parts because of the concentration and energy.'

Since he is at the stage where he can choose his work, especially with graphics, what will he choose? Where can he go from here? 'I now want to progress; this means money and expansion, and there are various options. One has either got to become a small business, no longer a one-man show, but get a partner with some capital, or, if you're not going to do that, you yourself have got to make yourself bigger and better because you're the product in a sense.' He has chosen not to become a businessman because 'I would have ended up behind a desk,' but to take the other path, 'in musical terms becoming a soloist rather than staying in an orchestra. I found that by aiming relatively low you don't take the risk of being rejected, but you get to the stage where you've classed yourself low on the professional ladder and therefore the financial returns are relatively low. OK you're super-efficient, you get it all done and you get a living at the end of the month, but you can't get any further because there isn't time, the wheels are spinning so fast, you can't do things on spec. I'm currently at the point of climbing out of that one.'.

Seven months later: 'In the next month I'm working on more ships coming from the Greeks; I've also contacted a dealer in ship's models and work may be coming from that. I've written an article on restoration for *Model Shipwright*, it's a good quarterly magazine. Really, things are continuing to get better.'

Part-time
Capital: tools cost about £200, of which the most expensive piece of equipment is a lathe, £100
no separate premises; one room used as workshop
Income: B
Formal qualifications: from art school

1980: 'Soon after I saw you last I was lying on a beach on Elba and got a "road-to-Damascus" that I would leave Guildford. In March '77 I moved to London and since then, apart from one graphics client, my work has been almost entirely ships modelling, half restoration and half yachts for owners and manufacturers. I got the job of building *ADC Accutrac*, Clare Francis's boat, for Capital Radio. A year later I saw in the paper that Operation Drake – *Eye of the Wind* – also involved Capital. So I went to see them, the first time I have ever initiated a deal. It took me four-and-a-half months to do, working in the evenings as well, but it's in the foyer now and it's beautiful. It gives off a certain energy.

'I'm doing another job for Capital which is a model of their studios. They sent for me and said, "We get a lot of kids coming round who want to see the studios and they can't except in little parties, so would you like to build a model." It is a honeycomb of studios, some of them very small; the model is up at an angle of forty-five degrees and you look through a window. There will be three pairs of headphones on the counter and Kenny Everett will give you a quick and racy rundown on how the studios operate.'

Jonathan T also completed a set of six caravan pictures which he sold outright to a publisher. He is currently working on a set of twelve horse-drawn fire-engines in use from the time of the Fire of London to 1900. 'I'm going to York to do one, which means measuring to the last nut and bolt and quite a lot of photography; it is a big old Victorian steamer with lots of pipes and knobs and bells. The history of the fire-brigade is completely wrapped up with the history of the insurance companies. They created the first fire-brigades in their own interest. I'm going to approach them and see if they could pay for the publication. They could produce a calendar with one a month. I'm not really worried how they go out, so long as the quality is high.'

Next in line is making a ship model on his own account. 'I've got to reverse the chain of command where you're always at the bottom of the chain. Once I build a model it exists, I decide on the price and somebody else is the client. I become the owner of a "work of art". I would need to sound out the market, but I also feel that if you make something which is amazing somebody is going to buy it, it's almost a natural law.

'There are two courses open to me. One is to get an apprentice, but by the nature of the work it's difficult to pass on. You either get somebody who isn't into it and he'll do it for a while until something better turns up or you get somebody and you teach them everything and they go. The other alternative is to become a "star". But what I've seen of the gallery world and the music world is that there are a lot of moons flying around stars. What I do want is to do something as well as it can possibly be done. Inevitably, that means you are doing it better than other people. I may not have the skills, economic conditions may not allow me, I might drop dead, not get to the top of the stairs, but I know what flight of stairs I'm on. If I do survive and get to be that good, and there is a market for what I'm doing, I would end up by being THE man. I'm happy about that now because it will happen organically. A few years ago a friend asked, "How would you like to be the greatest ship-modeller in the world?" and I said, "Oh, well . . ." because I didn't have the confidence.'

Full-time
Capital: electric fretsaw is an addition to his tools
Income: C/D (including nearly £1,000 for running occasional craft market in Guildford)

BEAUTY PRODUCTS
1980: Rona J and the three people who work with her make, fill, pack, label and dispatch her face creams, shampoos and hair conditioner from a kitchen-style factory in Edinburgh. Faith Products, starting six years ago in her Kircudbrightshire kitchen, has expanded into the kind of business which sells through much of Europe.

Rona J's face creams are made from rosemary leaves and camomile flowers, marigold petals and roses, honey, wheatgerm and Fuller's earth, 'top-quality BPC ingredients of vegetable nature. The creams are based on soya oil and the shampoos are a coconut derivative. All are pH-balanced favourably and do not contain any mineral oil (petroleum product) or harsh synthetics.' Faith Product's range is three moisturizers, one cleanser, one soft face masque, four shampoos and a hair conditioner.

Growing up in New York, Rona J took secretarial studies and book-keeping at high school, 'which became very important tools for me when starting a company', and went on to study psychology and sociology. Then, on a camping holiday in Canada, she found herself picking, tasting and drying herbs and looking into their mineral and vitamin content. As a vegetarian she had a particular interest in nutrition, which went well with an interest in herbs, and she made a healing ointment which was used successfully by friends on a variety of ailments.

In Scotland , where she came to live, Rona J soon noticed that her skin was getting very dry and that nothing she bought seemed to help. Other women, living nearby, had the same problem. A plant-based cream that succeeded in helping sensitive skins withstand the excesses of the Scottish winter was the result. Friends and relatives used it and sent back favourable reports. So, with one partner and £11, Rona J started her company from her cottage kitchen, devising the formulas, testing and mixing the creams, filling, boxing and casing the jars, handling all the mail orders, sales and books. They did everything in the kitchen, picking and pressing the plants growing round them. 'The philosophy behind the business was "need" essentially. I knew there was a real need for a good, pure product that could do the job. I saw so many pretentious things being marketed in fancy packages, I just wanted to get back to basic, simple, honest products.'

Moving to Edinburgh in 1975, Rona J employed an accountant to keep tabs on sales. By now she had given up her full-time job and had plunged into running her own business. Manufacturing was contracted out to an old-established herbal house in the north of England. 'With the factory it all got more impersonal – you lose the love a mother gives a child. But we lost nothing of the ingredients – they're the same as those that went into the kitchen sink.' Rona J supervised the factory to check that the products were up to standard; all the plants were grown on a nearby farm and the seaweed for shampoo was gathered not far away. She insists on strict safety standards and even puts products into her own eyes to test that they are not harmful. Her acceptance and recommendation by the Herb Society was, in her view, an accolade worth waiting for.

In June 1979 the company bought and moved into a small 'factory', with office attached, in Edinburgh. It is large enough to mix and fill all the creams; only the hair products are still contracted out and they will be brought to Edinburgh soon. Rona J, an employee of the company herself, also employs a full-time secretary, mixer and junior who mostly does the packaging and labelling but also helps with the mixing. She herself devises all the new recipes. 'I still do three people's jobs – advertising, books, ordering, wages and correspondence, sales . . .'

Starting with a few shops locally, Faith Products are now distributed (bulk and packaged) by carrier and post to most health-food shops and many wholefood shops in the UK and, under other companies' names, to Austria, France, Germany, Holland, Italy, Sweden and Singapore. 'I am hoping to sell to the USA, Australia and Japan quite soon. Now that we have FDA [Food and Drug Administration, USA] approval for the hair products and approval for the creams is on the way we should not have too much difficulty.' It wasn't all that easy six years ago, however; marketing was the most difficult side of the business. The product was unknown and, on Rona J's own admission, the packaging was all wrong. It was a matter of trial and error, advertising in health and hairdressing journals (which she still does occasionally) and carrying a sample case around. 'Now I no longer need to sell that way,' says Rona J. 'People come to us and I attend trade fairs – I've just got back from one in Paris and in Brighton.'

As well as the packaged range, there are bulk containers of five and twenty-five litres for shampoo and hair conditioner and of ten kilogrammes and upwards for face creams for refilling. The hairdressing trade uses Faith Products and so do beauty consultants.

The business continues to expand as the market does. Recipes are tested and developed and Rona J still forages for plants in the countryside. New recipes that work for a mass market, such as henna shampoo, find their way into the range. A pure vegetable, inexpensive soap and massage oil will shortly be introduced.

The future looks bright for Rona J, who has combined a practical business sense with a feeling for what was needed and mixed the two with a belief in her own product. 'It's really important for me to have a good product. I believe in fresh plants, made into fresh products in a balanced way – these have an honest value and are most effective.'

Full-time
Capital: £11 as a start
£13,000 approximately on employees' wages (including her own)
£2,500 approximately on machinery (stainless-steel mixer, filler and hob)
about £6,000 to £10,000 to set up the factory
Income: C/D
Formal qualifications: secretarial studies and book-keeping
Experience: in testing and using herbs

CHAPTER SEVEN

Eating & Entertaining

RESTAURANT

1976: Stephen J and his sister are running a wholefood snack bar in a university students' union. It is an *ad hoc* arrangement whereby they have the use of a large room with serving area and a back room with sinks for washing-up. 'The rest we had to find ourselves,' he says. 'We needed an oven, a fridge and something to boil the water up. The union financed these to the tune of £300 since we couldn't afford them straight off.'

Five months ago Stephen J gave up a teacher-training course to work with his sister, a wholefood cook of five years' standing; their only previous 'restaurant' experience was running a couple of stalls at pop festivals. With only three weeks to go before opening, they worked non-stop to get everything ready in time. Their list of essential jobs included: installing the cooker, buying crockery from jumble sales and second-hand shops, fitting locks on the doors, working out a menu, getting entry to a couple of cash-and-carrys (essential for bulk supplies of everything from cheese to plastic cups), stocking up on everything they could possibly need, ordering milk and bread and distributing small publicity posters. One day was spent finding and negotiating supplies from a greengrocer in the market. Food also came from a wholefood supplier in the town. They already had a van, which Stephen J says is essential, but chairs and tables were a problem; they made do with the low tables and easy chairs already in the room.

With everything ready they were in business. The first to come were the faithful organic few, 'members of the Whole Earth group', says Stephen J, 'who were pretty disgruntled about the university food'. The word spread that there was good food, music and a room with a view and now about two hundred people eat there every week. The snack bar, which is open over lunch-time during term, is manned by Stephen J and his sister and part-time student help. They have recently changed over to self-service because 'the queues were getting so ridiculous people had to wait twenty minutes before they got served. Self-service is a pretty miserable way of doing it but it's really efficient. It usually runs with two people behind the main counter doing hot foods and making sure all the salads are topped up, one person doing drinks – tea, coffee, fruit juice – and one person taking money at the end.'

Vicky J does all the cooking, mainly to her own recipes; the food includes well-tried favourites such as soups, vegetable stews, cauliflower cheese, savoury flans, apple pie, fruit cakes and specialities such as giant cookies. Prices work out at the cost of the food plus sixty per cent to cover expenses such as the van, wages and rent. 'It seems to be a pretty good formula,' says Stephen J. 'People are happy to come along and pay the prices and we're quite happy with the money that is coming in. It was a bit low at first, but now more people are coming.' Prices, though, are a contentious issue between him and some members of the union. Although their food is cheaper than cafés and vegetarian restaurants in the town, it is more expensive than the bar downstairs which also offers food and the snack bar upstairs which is run by the university at a loss and subsidized. But, says Stephen J, 'we're not prepared to run at a loss and ask somebody to subsidize us. Our argument is that if you don't like the prices you don't buy the food. If you don't buy the food we go out of business.'

When the lunch-time rush is over, most of the baking is done for the next day, so they usually finish around five or six unless they are catering for an evening function, such as a society's meeting. Most of the food buying is done at the weekend. 'That's one of my jobs', says

Stephen J, 'to drive the van and pick up all the supplies. Friday night is usually down to the cash-and-carry to stock up for the next week. Saturday morning we stick in an order with the greengrocer and pick it up in the afternoon. It's surprising how much work it takes, mainly because there are only two of us.'

Part of the work is peculiar to their surroundings. Since they share a washing-up room with the bar, everything has to be moved around and out again the next morning, especially after concerts or discos. The health inspectors from the local council are interested in all these arrangements and one of them came down a couple of weeks ago to look over the premises. 'You've got to have a reasonably clean set-up,' says Stephen J, 'and they look for first-aid boxes, clean floors, there's got to be no animals, insects or mice around. There are a few things he pointed out which we'll have to get over – one of these is glass shelving for covering the food.' Stephen J cannot just go out and 'buy shelving, it's too expensive. But they're reasonable people, they'll give us a fair time to do it and then come back and inspect.'

Health inspections aside, one of his irritations is the students' union or 'squabbles with the lefties' as he calls it. 'They don't like to see private enterprise going on under their noses. They want to know how much control they have over us and on the profit we're making.' As he sees it, if he drops his prices he either goes out of business like the vegetarian place downstairs which ran at a loss and left the union with a bill or he gets subsidized, which he is unwilling to see happen. 'The food has to be paid for in the end,' he says. The union complaint has nothing to do with him personally or the standard of the food, but much more with the fact that he is working for himself. Whether they stay or go 'depends on who gets in power next year. We're not interested in letting anybody control us, we'll just leave.'

Six months later: During the summer vacation the university union asked Stephen J to submit a tender for the snack bar. The union did not accept it. Then, two weeks into term, they offered the snack bar back to Stephen J. Meanwhile Vicky J had a job and he had a thriving business importing and distributing board games (another earlier interest). They might take up the offer, but everything is undecided at the moment.

Full-time (during term-time)
Capital: none
outlay on food £100 to £150 per week
casual help 50p to 60p an hour
£10 a week rent (approximately)
van essential
Income: A; other income from record stall, disco and importing board games
Formal qualifications: none
Experience: in cooking

Stephen J now imports and sells board games (see page 78).

PUB

1976: 'How about a pub when we retire?' Not a good idea, according to Michael K, the landlord of a pub in Oxford. Perhaps there are pubs down country lanes suitable for elderly but active couples, but on the whole pub life is as strenuous as any other, requiring considerable reserves of energy and stamina. 'Horses for courses' is a phrase which seems to fall off the tongue of anybody connected with the brewery trade: there's a pub for you if you can find it. Michael K found his after he and his wife looked at 130 others. 'There are many ways to go about getting a pub,' he says, 'but we went to a broker. As we didn't know anything about pubs we spent a long time looking at pubs all over the country. It was a useful exercise; the more we saw, the more we learnt.' They applied for three tenancies: the first one, in the wilds, would never have given them a living; the second one they missed through lack of experience; but the third one was just right – the brewery wanted a tenant with experience of students and Michael K had previously owned and run hostels for students.

Now with his wife, daughter, son, son-in-law, parents and staff he is running a large and busy pub. For the first four and a half years it was a tenancy, tied for supplies to one brewery; then Michael K bought the freehold from the brewery who were having distribution difficulties. Now it is a free house. What makes a good pub? Michael K is certain that 'it's a meeting point, a safety valve, people come to talk. When the door opens you've got to be ready, you've got to be ready to serve them. That's what it is about.' A lot of preparatory work goes on before the doors open. At half-past eight in the morning, he says, 'we talk about what we require in the way of food, what we need to buy. Then we get down here, let the staff in and if, like yesterday, I was minus four staff I have to start cutting sandwiches instead of going to the office.' At half-past ten the pub opens until half-past two; then there is a short breathing space until six, when it opens again until half-past ten or eleven on Fridays and Saturdays. After the last customer has gone there is still clearing up to be done. Most of the customers are students, college servants, workers from Cowley and, in the summer, tourists at lunch-time. It is a mixed group which seems to gel together, he says; the odd truculent one is dealt with by his wife. 'She handles the odd awkward customer very well,' he says, 'better than if I approached him.'

Michael K is fortunate in that he has a lot of family help. His wife and daughter do the cooking (cold buffet at lunch and grills in the evening), his son buys the wines, his son-in-law looks after VAT and similar duties and his parents are there in the morning. 'It makes it a lot easier for me because I can have holidays,' he says, 'which many publicans can't.' The catering side needs a lot of work. 'Food fluctuates so much,' he observes, 'that it is more difficult to handle than the wet side; it needs a lot of homework keeping up with the prices. Basically it comes down to portion control.' Although his pub is large, the same principle applies to any other pub which offers food. 'You have to suit your catering to the requirements of your customers,' he says. 'When we came here it was rather expensive so there wasn't much catering. We provided a cheaper meal and that did the trick.'

Although Michael K had no previous experience of pubs, he recommends working in one for both husband and wife before committing themselves. 'It's a lot harder than many people think,' he says, 'both physically and mentally. It can be demanding on family life, especially with young children.' Having decided that this is what they want, there are still a number of pitfalls which the brewery will point out at the interview for a tenancy. The main one is money. Buying a free house can cost from £27,000 to £30,000 upwards and even a tenancy is not cheap. The premium, a deposit which is held until the pub is vacated, can cost from £500 to £1,000 depending on turnover; ingoings, everything from lightbulbs to chairs, can either be a small amount or up to £10,000; working capital is also needed. Having found a tenancy, the new publican is very much his own boss in the day-to-day management of the pub within a broad framework laid down by the tenancy agreement. The brewery will inspect the premises now and again, especially for cleanliness. 'Cleanliness', says Michael K, 'is all-important. You have to clean everything religiously otherwise the beer is not going to be good. That is essential.'

Full-time
Capital: free house £27,000 to £30,000 upwards
  ingoings £10,000 or less
  tenancy premium from £500 to £1,000
  one full-time barman £40 to £50 a week
  family assistance
Income: C
Formal qualifications: none
Experience: owned and run hostels for students

1980: 'We still have the pub and it's run in the same way. We've introduced new beers, real-ale beers. We profess to have more real ales than any other pub in Oxfordshire.'

Full-time
Income: D

DISCOTHEQUE
1976: Peter B loved parties and this prompted him to devote £2,500 plus two years of evenings and weekends to researching, developing and building a discotheque and lighting system. It was originally intended to fit into a large suitcase. In practice it occupies a transit van and requires three-quarters of an hour and two strong men to set it up. It has cost him many friends (and many parties) through neglect and will never, he says, financially repay him. So why did he do it? 'It was just the interest of designing this mammoth thing,' he says, 'that eventually took over my life. It started when I was about eight or nine; my parents' record-player went wrong several times and I put it right. I sang in a choir and when my voice broke I collected albums and started building my own equipment. In the end I had to build a good disco just to satisfy myself.'

With no specialized knowledge of electronics, but with years of information garnering behind him, Peter B set to work. He decided on records rather than tapes (he had one hundred LPs at the time) and started the long haul of adding, subtracting and combining equipment until he arrived at the right sound. 'With a discotheque,' he says, 'you have to combine reliability, ruggedness, quality and portability. All these things are needed . . . I built everything twice, because things were either too heavy, too big, too small or didn't work. It's important to be able to update; very rarely do people get it right first time unless they've got endless amounts of money.'

For the timid there are other ways of setting up the hardware: buy a proprietary system (£100 to £800 without lighting); buy parts from different systems to get a suitable combination; buy a second-hand system from retailers or watch *Exchange & Mart*. Before buying anything, check it over thoroughly. Read hi-fi magazines. With a little wood-working ability a good alternative to DIY is to buy the separate parts and construct matching cases. Whatever is chosen will have to fit into a small area for private parties as well as catering for a larger space. Peter B aims to be adaptable. For a recent party he only used part of his equipment in a smallish room. But the most important thing, says Peter B, is to look after the records.

Now that he has completed and tested the equipment, he has to sell the product. To date he has had three gigs, all friends, and the disco has worked perfectly. He has advertised in *Time Out*, *Melody Maker* and *Record Mirror* and intends to advertise in the up-market *Harper's and Queen*. It is obviously evening work and his prices run from £10 to £15, depending on what people can afford; that price has to cover expenses such as petrol and insurance.

For the moment, at least, Peter B will continue working as an engineer during the day and join the eight to ten thousand part-time disco operators in the country. 'I've had a couple of offers to take the disco to Germany,' he says, 'but it means amazing insurance problems. The other thing I could do is to go into a town with a lot of young people, hire a hall, charge 30p or 40p a head, do a Friday and Saturday night show and move on.'

Seven months later: During the summer Peter B has been working a disco on riverboats up and down the Thames. 'It's a well-trodden course,' he says, 'but it only lasts during the summer. I've discovered that advertising is not worthwhile. Now I intend to contact all the local and sports' clubs within a fifteen-mile radius, that's about four to five hundred clubs, offering regular gigs at their social and fund-raising events. For anybody starting out I've also discovered that it's much better to begin very simply, just as you would with hi-fi, and then add on as you need it.'

Part-time
Capital: £2,500 on equipment
  van essential
  no separate premises
Income: A
Formal qualifications: as engineer

1980: Peter B works full-time as an engineer and when he found himself travelling away from home and not being able to commit himself he gave up the disco. 'It was really a hobby for me. The people I got to stand in for me didn't always do a good job and also I had all my equipment stolen.

'It was an interesting exercise and I learnt a lot – mainly about communication with people. I found that you have to listen to the client's requirements. The impression I got was that many people had difficulties with the disc jockey: he'd play too loud or not what they wanted, there's a lot of ego in this type of work. Disc jockeys tend to put on the kind of show they want and there's not much consideration for the client.'

PUPPETRY

1976: A man who has had sixty different jobs in his life, Derek C intends to play Punch and Judy until he is ninety. He grew towards puppetry after ten years' acting and it developed from making his first papier-mâché puppets to putting on shows in the Edinburgh theatres. Then, while acting in a dreary pantomime season, he said to himself, 'I shall never take on another part which I don't want to do,' and that decision, he says, was a big step. 'I didn't know how I was going to live, how I was going to support myself. I had started the Punch and Judy and was getting the odd booking. I became self-employed. As an actor one is always self-employed but this was different; I had to start learning how to promote myself, get shows together, write scripts and so on, things which I had never done.' Derek C kept the Punch and Judy show and developed others, including one called *Tales of King Arthur* which was written by his girlfriend. He discovered, not for the first time, that puppetry needed all his skills: 'Carpentry, tailoring, sculpting, everything came into making this production,' he says.

Although he is still taking the occasional acting part, Derek C is committed to puppetry. 'It can show all things at once,' he says. 'With Punch and Judy there are sixteen characters that I use. It's like the Tarot cards, they're aspects of yourself. Punch is the male aspect, Judy is the female aspect. It's a very moral tale; its roots lie right back in the mummers' plays.'

Now living in London Derek C has to start afresh, building up new contacts. 'As a performer you have to be seen,' he says, 'otherwise you don't work.' He plays to both adult and child audiences, but his favoured age group is the three to five-year-olds. 'The enjoyment comes from the less sophisticated part of the mind,' he says, 'and I've discovered that working with children because they respond immediately.' London is rather overstocked with puppeteers, he finds, and his fee has dropped from a dependable £20 to as little as £15. Apart from theatre bookings, Derek C busks on the streets and entertains for birthday parties, pre-school playgroups and community groups, anywhere where there is an audience. He makes puppets for sale and teaches in children's workshops. In the summer Derek C and his dog will tour parks in Glasgow, Edinburgh and Dundee, playing from his purpose-built van. 'The idea of the show is that you're complete,' he says. 'I arrive and the show can start the second I get there. The van has a power supply, I can eat and sleep in it. It has two tape recorders, lighting and a drop-down stage. It's an old system, working out of doors in parks. You're competing with traffic, road drills and all sorts of distractions, but it's very rewarding because you get a mixed audience.'

In Edinburgh he was working with others; now he is virtually on his own and at times it is quite a strain. 'I find discipline is difficult to find,' he says, 'and difficult to maintain. You've got to be infinitely variable and resilient. If you can't paint the van because it is raining you've got to come in here and do something else. You can waste an awful lot of time worrying what to do instead of getting on with it.' Another thing, he says, is that 'if you're on your own you're constantly drawing on your own resources; you write the play, direct it, produce it and publicize it'. Once, after a depressing period without bookings, he went round to the labour exchange looking for a job – any job – but he discovered 'there is no way back. Once you know what you want to do, and I believe most people know, you just follow that.'

Six months later: 'The Scottish tour went well,' says Derek C. 'I did seventy-five shows in six weeks. I'm soon off to South Hill Park community arts centre for six months where I'll be part of a little company of three people who I worked with in Edinburgh. We'll be "actors and actresses in residence", I think we are called. We shall be doing cabaret, pub shows and some puppetry. I hope to get a show of *Under Milk Wood* organized; it will be a big job, there will be fifty to sixty puppets.'

Full-time
Capital: one puppet costs about £1.50 to £2
van essential; equipped as 'theatre' cost £400
no separate premises
Income: A
Formal qualifications: none
Experience: in acting, sculpting, tailoring, carpentry

1980: Derek C's repertoire now includes clowning: unicyling, juggling and his star piece, a clown car. For the uninitiated, a clown car is an unorthodox automobile which sprouts wings, squirts water, loses its doors and then explodes, all to the accompaniment of loud bangs and horn-tooting. It is very popular with children. 'With the clown car,' he says, 'I've had audiences up to 2,000 and been with it on stage as well as in the open. I've been to Oslo with the clown car, done two shows a day in Greenwich Park and taken it to the Riverside Studios. For a community arts event, for example, I could do twenty to thirty minutes of clown car, ending up with Punch and Judy.'

After his successful stint at South Hill Park, Derek C bought his first clown car and he's been working with one ever since. He continues to offer Punch and Judy, mostly for children, though a family audience is good because each age group helps the other: 'The children laugh quite naturally and the adults help the children to respond to the word-play. I'm always trying to find new ways to do things. For the last few years I've done a Christmas show for Heals and it has to be a bit different every year. People trust what I do

– they ring me up and ask me what I would like to do and I make up things for different situations.'

Since the end of summer 1979 Derek C's work, like many other businesses, has been slow. He doesn't advertise much or sit around waiting for the phone to ring. 'I can't be inactive. I've been repairing cars and I've had experience restoring my house, so I've got electrical, plumbing and building skills which I can put to good use' – which he does. He is also attending drama classes at Riverside, working with professionals and taking small parts on television – but, again, only those which he wants to do.

With a number of strings to his bow – which he draws on – Derek C says his life is less fraught. 'Discipline is no longer a problem. I'm better at the business side of it and I know how to launch a publicity campaign. I don't charge a definite price for what I do because some people have more money and some have less. It's important, though, to get a good price otherwise you feel mean in performance. My fees have gone up of course. It's sometimes difficult to explain to somebody why you are charging more this year than last. It's not just inflation, it's also that I am doing a better show and providing more – such as the juggling. Nobody pays me to learn juggling and yet it's something else that I can offer.

'It's important for me to use all my skills, whether for a pre-school playgroup or for an audience of thousands. That's the way to move forward and moving forward is important.'

Full-time
Income: C (£4–5,000; 'all my money goes back into the business – I've just spend £1,000 on new equipment')

ACTING
See page 166–67.
ENTERTAINING IN A RESTAURANT
See page 3.

CHAPTER EIGHT

Services

HAIRDRESSING

1976: People are very fussy about their hair and the way it is cut. They can be even fussier about who cuts it. A good haircut makes all the difference.

Sharon M cuts hair at home. Trained on a six-month course with Vidal Sassoon, she worked in the salon for a while, then left to make wigs and work as a secretary – having nothing to do with hairdressing at all, except when friends came for haircuts. Three years ago one of them said, 'Why on earth don't you do freelance work?' so she did. 'When I started,' she says, 'I advertised in *Time Out*, which seemed to bring in the right type of people, people who didn't like going to salons, being pushed around, not given proper attention, all the hustle and bustle. Some people rather like that, others don't like it at all.'

Sharon M still advertises, but most of her clients now come by word-of-mouth. 'It's very enjoyable from that point of view,' she says. 'I probably know many of my clients quite well and that takes a bit of time to build up.' Advertising can have its problems. 'You can get some very strange phone calls,' says Sharon M, 'so I put ''genuine callers only'' and that cut down most of the odd people. You need an intercom system on the door at least so you can sound people out. If you're a woman and you're dealing with men you've got to be very careful. It depends on your attitude. If you keep at a distance you're fine, I don't think there's any problem.'

Initially, Sharon M relied on an answering service which, as well as protecting her from unwelcome phone calls, 'had a diary for me so they made all my appointments; that was marvellous because it meant that I didn't have to discipline myself, I was almost being run by my agent'. Now married and about to move to a new flat, Sharon M is making her own appointments in a different market. She is hoping to reduce the number of individual clients and make visiting family appointments instead. 'I'm trying to set up home visits,' she says, 'going out to people, the woman at home with children who can't get out to the salon. After a time you get fed up being in the same place all the time and it's good for me because it means I can get out. I had a family yesterday, two next-door neighbours and two children. So I did the four of them in one go.' Her new flat has a spare room which 'I'm going to turn into a salon with a proper floor, a basin in there so I can shut the door on it. You really need to. With people walking round you don't feel as if it's your home any more.' For all that, a simple wash, cut and blow dry – which is what Sharon M gives – needs little space or equipment: scissors, brushes, hairdriers ('I've got three in case one goes wrong'). She charges £5. 'You have to find a middle-of-the-road price,' she says. 'I haven't put up my price for two years but I notice people thinking twice about paying £5 for a haircut. At the moment I'm not very busy and I know that my hairdresser isn't very busy. It's all to do with the climate of the times, money is tight. It just depends how people look at it, how they value it.' Hairdressers' charges are very different around the country: in London £5 for a haircut is quite reasonable. It gives Sharon M a good living even though she never knows from week to week, even from day to day, how busy she will be. She might not work at all, she might cut six people's hair. It can be very demanding. Good training is obviously invaluable because 'it gives you the confidence to see through what you're going to do with the hair. If you've got good training that carries you through because you get all sorts of reactions from people. I've had people walk out crying and the next day ring me up and say, ''I'm sorry, it's marvellous,'' and that kind of thing is quite upsetting. This is where confidence in the work and the standard really carries me through.'

Eight months later: 'I've kept some of my old clients,' says Sharon M, 'but I'm doing more home visits now. I've also started cutting hair in the evening, some people seem to prefer that . . . It makes a great difference having the extra room in the flat, I can go in there and shut the door. It's far less disturbing.'

Part-time
Capital: none
  hairdriers cost between £10 and £20
  the 'salon' in her flat cost £100 for the floor and £20 for the sink
Income: A
Formal qualifications: six-month course at Vidal Sassoon
Experience: previous employment

1980: Sharon M had a baby and is cutting the hair of her neighbours and their children only.

MIDWIFERY

1980: Hazel S delivers babies in the home. Until recently this was an unusual event – but now, for many women, a normal delivery at home is a natural alternative to the labour ward of a hospital. There are community midwives, of course, who are attached to the NHS, but Hazel S and her partner Marianne offer a freelance service. 'The main reason why people come to us', she says, 'is because they know who their midwife is going to be. They want friendship, some kind of personal relationship. We've come into their house, we've drunk their tea and we've talked to them. We're providing a service that has been pushed out by the nuclear set-up, the lack of extended family. We provide some kind of continuity. People don't often realize that, whoever your midwife is, you'll end up having a deep relationship with her. The birth just opens everybody wide apart, you relate to people directly, emotionally and personally.' Hazel S freely admits that this care can also come from the community midwives, but most of them are worked off their feet.

Hazel S and her partner offer time and the ability to smooth the way through the system. 'We have to organize the situation for them. You find out what they want, whether they are frightened of hospitals, they have other children they don't want to leave, they are sick of officialdom; usually it's upper-middle-class or middle-class people who've got some money and can afford to take on a private person.' The women who come to them have usually been well screened by the medical services, but often Hazel S has to find a doctor who will attend the birth and, as often, she mediates between GP and patient.

Only about half her mothers have had babies before. 'Having babies is a very frightening time,' she says. 'The actual birth and the post-natal period is very disturbing. You don't know what's happening to you. If you're a well-balanced person with a solid home situation and a good relationship you won't have any trouble coping with your pregnancy. You'll be able to deal with things that come along. But if any of those factors are missing . . . We do get unsupported mothers. We provide certain things that they wouldn't necessarily get from the ordinary midwife who comes into their home in a uniform, does the things that a midwife does and goes away again; we come to them for longer, talk to them more, maybe go a bit deeper.'

Midwifery is more than delivering babies. 'Any fool can deliver a baby,' midwifery students are told, but there's all the before-and-after care. One day a week Hazel and Marianne hold a clinic in Marianne's house. 'Expectant mothers come and we take a full history: obstetric history, medical history, family history, social history – enough to know what sort of person they are, whether they are fit or not. We see them monthly to twenty-eight weeks, then fortnightly to thirty-six weeks, then weekly to term. We see them for an hour in the clinic.'

Marianne and Hazel take it in turns to see patients at the clinic and in turn to do home visits; this way they can exchange information and views. 'You need somebody to cover you. I had two deliveries on Saturday and I was exhausted and Marianne was able to cover me on Sunday. Above everything, you have to want to be a midwife, above all personal desires and needs.' After the first birth on Saturday Hazel S went home to do the shopping and 'got bleeped for my other lady . . . I just had to do it. I could not have gone home and said, "No, I'm not going to do it." How can you not go? She needs me.'

When Hazel S gets to the mother's home and finds her in labour she rings the GP and tells him what is happening. Most of her births are problem-free and, so far, Hazel S has experienced no maternal or foetal deaths. 'The rate of that happening is very low. The more we do, the more chances there are of coming up against a catastrophe. You tend, as the midwife, to be full of yourself but there is a common adage that "Obstetrics would make a fool of you," and you know that you can't be too smart about anything.

'You never do know until it's all over and done, until you've discharged them, you really don't know what's going to happen. The birth is going along OK and the baby comes out. Is it going to breathe? Breathing fine. If it doesn't breathe then you've got to move quickly, you've got to clear away the mucus, make sure the airways are clear, warm it, stimulate it and make sure it gets oxygen into its lungs as soon as possible.'

Has she ever had to rush mother and baby off to hospital?

'Yes, but it's not usually in a rush. There are three things that can happen. Either the baby, when it comes out, doesn't breathe – you can deal with that. I have intubation equipment, oxygen and my own ability. Or the mother may bleed. If she does that you've got the same equipment as in a hospital. You've got intravenous ergometrine . . . which you give immediately you see that she's bleeding more than she ought to be. If the placenta is still in you ring the Flying Squad and they're on their way.

'The other reason for going to hospital is when you have some kind of obstruction. The baby gets wedged in the pelvis, the head is the wrong way round or the contractions die off. That's not usually dangerous. It would lead to maternal exhaustion and foetal distress. A labour that happens in a straightforward way just happens. Anything that is starting to cause a hold-up . . . you ring the hospital, get the ambulance and in you go.'

But most of the births are straightforward enough. After the baby is born, Hazel S gathers her equipment, examines the placenta, makes sure the mother is not bleeding and the baby is well. Then the mother, child and father are left alone to savour the experience. 'Labour is strenuous and arduous and exhausting so you need a lot of support, but you don't want to interfere with the post-partum stage where everybody is blissed-out.'

The baby is weighed and a nappy put on, the cord tied off and the mother put in a bath. The baby has already been put to the breast, as soon after birth as possible. Then, having checked the mother's temperature, blood pressure, pulse and uterus she goes away, to call again a few hours later, then twice daily for three days and daily for at least ten days. Post-natal clinics follow as a matter of course.

Although freelance, all midwives have to be registered. Hazel S notifies her local health-authority supervisor of her intention to practise and of her patients in the district, sends discharge forms and adheres to any screening requirements. She works closely with the woman's GP and advises expectant mothers to take their vitamins and do their exercises – among many other things – often under the aegis of the National Childbirth Trust. Despite a certain suspicion of freelance midwives, women will often be referred by GPs, community midwives and others in the NHS.

As well as being dedicated, a midwife needs to be strong, adaptable and meticulous. There are records to be kept straight and tests to be done. 'But the main problem is that you're with the patient until it is all over. It's not necessarily a problem but, in a long-drawn-out birth, you get very worn-out. Basically, you're in sole charge of the patient and her emotional state and your emotional state and her husband's emotional state. You have to know what you're doing, you must be quite a good midwife, you can't take it on lightly . . . It makes it worthwhile when you have a happy mother and a happy delivery.'

Full-time
Capital: for equipment, perhaps £1,000
car essential; also radio-pager
Income: £175 to £200 per birth inclusive of all care ('although we will accept £50 from an unsupported mother'); ten to twelve births a month maximum for partnership of two or three
Formal qualifications: State Certified Midwife (or Integrated Course; nursing plus midwifery)
Experience: in labour wards and special-care baby unit

ACUPUNCTURE

1980: 'Traditional acupuncture', says David A, 'deals with the flow of energy that circulates through us, through nature. The flow has been mapped out by the ancient Chinese on charts and it's an established system and a very old one too. The theory is that this flow of energy should be harmonious, should be unimpeded and there shouldn't be any blockages. When it is that way you are a fully integrated person and you are healthy in mind, body and spirit. If that flow is interrupted for some reason, if it's not harmonious, then you open yourself up to disease on a spiritual, mental or physical level.'

Acupuncturists still follow that tradition and there are one or two colleges in the country that teach it. It was disillusion with his profession as an architect and a bad back that led David A to acupuncture. 'I was treated by an osteopath and I really liked what the guy was doing. It fired me. It was the notion of applying your hands on someone and soothing pain. I found a massage course, though it took a year or two for that intention to come to fruition.'

He worked during the day and went to classes in the evening. He bought a couch and was able to treat friends and people in the office who knew he was good with bad backs. 'I felt very strongly that I could be a therapist. At the same time I realized there was something too superficial about massage. You were able to calm someone, bring relief from pain, but it didn't really get to the root of the problem. I talked to friends and read books and this notion of energy came about. From there acupuncture.'

David A continued working as an architect during the day and studying in the evenings and at weekends. After one or two false starts, he arrived at the College of Traditional Chinese Acupuncture in Leamington Spa. At the end of 1975 he left his job and, as he was an associate, he received a year's salary and kept the car.

'I was wanting to give up but I was scared of the jump. I was putting out the feeling that I wanted to leave without saying so until, one day, my boss said to me, "Your heart isn't in this, is it?" and I could only say that that was quite true. I might have quit earlier, but I had a divorced wife and child to support throughout. That made me cagey about having some security.'

David A was not concerned about making a good income. 'I was quite happy to make ends meet because I do live rather frugally. I'm much happier with the little car and the bicycle.'

What was the difficulty?

'Fear of the unknown,' he says. 'There had always been the security of the pay packet at the end of the month. It was a very strange feeling not having to go to work – being master of every minute of my day – not having any patients at all for the first month. In fact, I didn't have an acupuncture qualification then, I had about six months until I qualified, so I got busy setting up a massage practice. I went round shops and local chemists and let it be known that I was available to give massage. It worked, a few patients started coming. The massage had to be local because it's the best form of growth, setting up roots where you live, where people can see you every day.'

In September he finished the clinical part of the training, received his qualification and acupuncture patients started arriving. The first patients were referred by the college. 'The work is such', he says, 'that each patient seems to recommend another one. The quality of the work and the quality of the care is such that you are never wanting for patients. I would like to use this practise as a facility for newcomers who can work here and take on patients, because I have quite a backlog.'

If acupuncturists are flourishing, is the medical profession doing its job? David A thinks it isn't as clear-cut as all that. 'Most of my patients have been through the usual channels and have had little joy. I'm not putting down doctors at all, we all work for the patient's good. Unfortunately, GPs are lumbered with so many patients that they can sometimes give only five minutes to each one.

'It's in the nature of the work that you have to know your patients well to find the cause of the problem, to know how to treat. This is what we're working on, we're trying to find the cause of the problem which results in certain symptoms of physical, mental or spiritual illness.'

Are people ever cured?

'You're treating them as individuals really, you're not treating their problem. The essence of traditional acupuncture is to find the cause of that problem at energy level and to bring about a change in the circulation of energies; you find that the symptoms wane and gradually disappear.'

A prospective patient is first asked for a life and medical history (case-taking) plus some rather unusual questions, such as his favourite colour. It is an opportunity for people to unburden themselves and for the acupuncturist to listen. This is followed by taking the pulses (several on each wrist), which diagnose the state of the elements and the major organs. Moxa, a herb, may be burnt and fine needles inserted at critical points – these may act as an input of energy or as a means of unlocking a 'knot'. At all stages, the pulses are consulted. There is of course the rather better-known acupuncture technique which acts as an anaesthetic. 'It's similar to a doctor giving a pain-killer. If a patient is obsessed with pain, then the fact of being relieved of it may assist with the healing process.'

Although licensed to practise, David A has not finished his training. He is working towards his doctorate and, at the same time, teaching students at the college and taking small practical classes at home. Students go to Leamington once a month for a long weekend, have homework to do, including reading ten pulses a day, and exams to pass. David A says, 'We're really lucky to have Professor Worsley as our teacher. He's imparting a quality of life which stimulates one to learn and become more aware. It's a way of developing as a person. There is this joy and wanting to go out and treat.'

Full-time (one weekday off but sometimes working at weekends, in the early morning and evenings)
Capital: none
no separate premises
Equipment: room, couch, blanket, books, charts, moxa, lighter, needles and appointment book
Income: £7 an hour-long session, except for case-taking which is £14
Formal qualifications: Licentiate in Traditional Chinese Acupuncture
David A is Bachelor in Acupuncture

TOURIST GUIDE

1976: Many tourists manage to get around on their own perfectly well. Other tourists prefer to sightsee surrounded by their compatriots and escorted by a guide who, besides shepherding them in and out of their coaches, will be a walking encyclopaedia, full of English history and information on museums, pubs, transport, theatres and shopping. Paul S is one such guide. During the season from April to September he is on call as a London guide, ferrying tourists around London and anywhere within a day's drive: Stratford, Oxford, Cambridge, Canterbury, Windsor. His services officially cost £15 a day, the rate laid down by the Guild of Guide Lecturers which is campaigning for the full rate for qualified guides and the withdrawal of undercutting unqualified guides. It is a controversial subject. The London Tourist Board, for example, runs a six-month qualifying course, but travel agencies and others also employ unqualified guides for less pay. There are other courses around the country and an aspiring guide should go on one if possible. Paul S says so and he has been a qualified guide for two years.

For six months of the year Paul S, if he is lucky, will be worked off his feet; for the rest of the year he will be virtually unemployed, except for the antiques business which supplements his income. Work comes through the Guild (which acts as his agent), the LTB or personal recommendation. It is a job which demands the endurance and patience of an elephant and the capacity to answer never-ending curious questions. 'A guide', says Paul S, 'has to be calm, has to be kind. It could be summed up in "be kind".' It also helps to be fluent in a modern language or two and to have the instincts of a teacher, 'to enjoy absorbing knowledge and giving it out again', he says. 'It's rather like teaching in that way.'

As well as tourists, Paul S takes round groups of businessmen on conferences, 'with a couple of days free for visits. Or I pick them up from the airport, take them around for a day or two and drive them back to the airport.' Business trips can mean extra research for the guide, as when 'a group of Americans were coming over in June to look at the docks – the whole area up for redevelopment – and I wrote off to the Ministry asking for information. There are things like this which you have to do for yourself.' Most of his work is with tourists, usually American or European. 'There are three types of American tourist,' Paul S says. 'There is the rich man coming to this country who really wants to get to know it. He probably buys a house and stays some time. The next kind comes over for two to three weeks. The first stop will probably be Shannon, round the ring of Kerry, to Dublin, Glasgow or Edinburgh, followed by the Lakes or York, North Wales, Heart of England, Bath and London. The third type is on a grand tour of Europe and comes to London for three or four days. He'll go on day trips and be booked into the Palladium, a theatre or a night club.' And the European tourist? 'Much more discerning. Germans are particularly good tourists, they want to know what makes this place tick. The French don't always like each other, never mind liking us. The Italians find it difficult to get money out of their country but they manage to come somehow. Of course, now the pound is falling England is a very attractive place for Europeans and they come to buy.'

Part-time (six months of year)
Capital: none

Income: B
Formal qualifications: London Tourist Board Guide badge (see regional tourist boards for information)
one or two European languages

1980: Paul S is living in America and planning to bring groups interested in antiques over to Britain. The pound is strong at the moment, which makes the UK more expensive than formerly for tourists, but they still come.

The LTB official rate per day is £30+.

MINI-CABS

1976: David B had a brilliant career as an opera singer; he was in full flood when, at the age of twenty-four, he woke up one day to find his voice had disappeared. 'The voice was in shreds,' he says. 'It was a dreadful time, a singer without a voice is a desolate creature.' With a family to support, 'I thought, well, pull out some of your other resources'. He sold vacuum cleaners. He went into acting. 'I did everything but sing for six or seven years. I did rep. for a year, I did old-time music hall, I was the third man in a knockabout busking act. I worked in West End musicals, I did television, never sang a note.' He also ran a decorating business and sold insurance. 'To work for yourself you've got to want to do it very much,' he says, 'because, although you get all the credits, all the benefits, there's nowhere the buck can go, the buck stops here, whether it's financially, artistically, no matter what.'

The voice came back, opera work came back, but nevertheless 'it was a blessing when my voice disappeared because it gave me enormous strength and resourcefulness,' he says. 'Once upon a time I would have sat down and cried. But you become resilient, you can work your way round things.' Nowadays David B only accepts the roles he wants to sing. 'I would rather be independent of theatre work so I have this little business.'

This little business is the mini-cab firm which he and his three partners started six months ago. All the partners have previously worked as mini-cab drivers. 'I initially started working as a mini-cab driver so I could get off for rehearsals,' he says. 'One has to have a four-door car which is reasonably new. But I was getting into a rut because I had to conform to the hours which the guv'nor wanted me to.' When he and his partners found an office they left to start up on their own. David B is the only one with another occupation – singing – and that comes first; the business fits round it, but it is in no way just a standby job. 'In many ways I'm very business conscious,' he says. 'I like doing the things which use me up. I still work quite hard but I work the hours that suit me.' The partners all cover different aspects. 'I'm the trouble-shooter,' David B says, 'I sort out the problems, do the finances, administration, try to get contracts. Someone else engages the drivers, another one sorts out the cars if they have problems. Another person is there basically to do long hours.' They all do some driving, picking up people and parcels. 'We are the alternative service, quite a different function from the black cab. We'll go anywhere, go long distances, book in advance, doesn't matter. We also do light removals by van.' There are a few regulations governing the use of mini-cabs: one of these is a requirement to keep the car looking like any other, i.e. no lights, phone numbers or notices. The abuse of this law by mini-cab firms gets the regular taxi service up in arms. 'Of course the black cabs are justified in grousing,' says David B. 'They spend a year or two learning routes; it's hard graft and it's expensive. They're entitled to the privileges that they have. There is a place for both.'

Back in the office the controller sits by the telephone taking orders during the day and night. Each driver supplies his own car, insured for 'Hire and Reward' (£80 upwards), and pays the office a commission on his fare of 25p a mile. The business thus acts like an agency. Each partner keeps his own driving money and the drivers' commission initially pays the office expenses, including the wages of the controller. The GPO, predictably slow, will not be giving them a radio line for another six months.

David B finds clients. 'I do a soft, careful sell,' he says. 'There's not much passing trade so we have regular clients. We do deliveries for factories; we also do all the work for some public houses and individuals. The first call a person makes is the time to consolidate the business; they must become one of your customers.' The way to retain a customer is good service: good driving, time-keeping, presentable car and driver, not overcharging. David B insists his drivers open the car door. 'The critical thing,' he says, 'is "Will they be looked after?" If you can supply that, you'll have them coming back again and again. For example, yesterday evening there was a collection of teenage girls who go to dances and who all come back to the same area. They won't get a driver who is either going to overcharge them or play about with them. They know they're going to be all right.'

Eight months later: The mini-cab business is improving all the time and getting a name for itself in North London. As a result, the two partners (reduced from four) are getting less pub work and more better paid work, such as contracts for driving to and from the airport. They have recently bought the lease of their premises and have settled in.

Full-time at the moment
Capital: £150 from each partner at the beginning
  £750 a year rent for premises
  £22 a week for part-time controllers
  £70 a week covers overheads such as rent, wages of controllers, phone, electricity (the drivers' commission is about £60 a week)
  four-door saloon car; one driver has van
Income: C
Formal qualifications: driving licence
Experience: working for a mini-cab firm

1980: David B has given up his share in the mini-cab business because he found that he couldn't work in harmony with his partner and because his theatre work – the real love of his life – was expanding. For the last two-and-a-half years he has been very busy singing and acting: the lead in *Under the Greenwood Tree* at the Vaudeville, in *Much Ado About Nothing* in Salisbury, followed by eight months at the Old Vic. Now he is doing auditions, meeting casting directors and waiting for the right offer.

'I'm taking an entrepreneurial gamble. I have my own little business, my own little business is myself. It's a terrifying time in a way because I'm turning work down, work that I could have done two years ago but now the status is not right, the salary is not right. To take a simple example: if you're a plumber you don't work as a plumber's mate. I'm very fresh to the scene in many ways, which is a disadvantage because when I go for auditions I'm up against household names. For the theatre I keep the status intact by not going below it; as soon as I go below it I have to renegotiate fees, you're back to square one. I'm pushing for higher stakes without a great deal of financial background and putting myself deliberately on a limb, which is something a forty-year-old man wouldn't do unless there was something driving him – he would settle for comfort and security.

'There is no fixed salary coming in and there are certain commitments to meet. I'm hoping I can afford to pay the self-employed pension I have just taken out. This will be a time when I can paint the house and do a bit more mini-cabbing. It's much better for me to do something completely out of the theatre rather than jeopardize my position in it.'

David B likes work and more work. If it wasn't for the theatre and opera he wouldn't mind doing anything. 'There's no amount of government legislation will stand in your way if you really want to do something.'

DISPATCH SERVICE

1979: 'I had this idea of making a fortune,' says John D, who must be one of the youngest entrepreneurs in the country. 'When I was seventeen I bought a motorbike, had a holiday job with a large dispatch firm, saw how inefficient they were and thought I could do better.'

Leaving school at seventeen he started a dispatch firm with his brother Mark who had just left university. With £5,000 in his pocket, he spent £2,000 on setting up an office in Islington. In the early days they did all the riding themselves and a friend was employed to answer the telephone. Later, ten riders, all self-employed, joined them.

All went well until Mark had a bad accident and was rushed to hospital with a crushed leg. 'I had the choice of closing down or going on by myself,' says John D. 'I was eighteen at the time and felt very much on my own. I depended on Mark a lot, he did all the VAT for example, but I decided to go on.' However, although he had fifty clients by the summer of 1979, he got bored, couldn't expand because he didn't have the capital, and decided to sell.

Another dispatch firm bought him out and John D started a garage with one of his riders. It has not been an unqualified success. For a start he doesn't like getting his hands dirty. He financed it, did the paperwork and book-keeping and his partner did the mechanics. That lasted four months.

John D kept in touch with the man who bought his firm. 'I get on well with him and we decided we could start another dispatch service. He hasn't got the time and was looking for someone with experience. We decided to go into it on a big scale with lots of advertising, letters and cards to all the big West End companies. He'll own fifty-one per cent and I'll own forty-nine per cent of the shares.'

Why set up another company?

'He doesn't have time to do any more work. It's an expanding market and there will be a bigger firm as support. Another reason is that everybody changes their dispatch service from time to time – you can only be efficient so far. On a Friday evening in the rush hour, when everybody wants something delivered, you're bound not to be completely efficient.'

Friday evenings apart, what makes for a good service?

'A good voice at the other end of the phone,' John D says. 'That's very important. Also efficiency – we shall be helped by the parent company which can both absorb surplus work we may have and also give us work.'

A dispatch service finds its market, he says, in the inefficiency of the Post Office. 'Clients are usually publishers, solicitors, travel agencies, advertising agencies. People use us when they want something delivered quickly or when they can't trust it to the post – such as a precious manuscript. My mother tells me that there used to be four deliveries of mail a day. I believe that it is still illegal to deliver a letter. The Post Office has started its own dispatch service, but that's inefficient too.'

Why did he decide to work for himself?

'My family are academic and I felt left out. I wanted to do something creative like starting firms. I don't like being told what to do and I would find it impossible to be employed. I work very hard when I'm interested. Towards the end of the last company I let it run by itself and my manager lost me a lot of money. I've learnt that, to run your own business, you have to have a finger in everything, you have to know what's going on.'

Being so young, there's an element of self-protection here. John D covers up the fact that he's only twenty and lives at home. 'I keep my private life and my work quite separate. Riders would lose respect for me if they knew I was only twenty and lived at home. They don't have to like me but they must respect me, must know I am boss. I have to make the decisions if it's to run efficiently.'

Full-time
Capital: £2,000 for rent of office, telephones, stationery and two motorbikes; riders need radio-pager
Income: riders can earn £100 a week if they work hard
clients are charged £1.60 flat rate plus 65p for each postal district the rider passes through; 40p a mile for long distances
John D's income: A
Formal qualifications: none
Experience: previous employment with dispatch firm; half an hour with mother's accountant learning how to keep the books

Six months later: John D's plans got snarled up by the Post Office. 'The idea was to get our name – Bow Street Runners – well known and grow at a rapid rate with the back-up of a large firm behind us with plenty of bite and plenty of money.' The Post Office said they would take eleven months to put in the telephones. With commendable initiative, John D wrote to Sir Keith Joseph and the phones were installed in a matter of weeks. Even so, the new company missed the winter weather which, it had been hoped, would bring in business (competitors being less efficient in ice and snow).

At the beginning of March, Bow Street Runners went into operation. The 6,000 letters they sent out to major West End companies 'met with an incredibly poor response. It ended up with me having to go round to clients talking to them and telling them what a wonderful firm we are and putting cards in people's letter-boxes. Anyone I hear about who might use us I zip over and talk to them. I hate selling, going to someone's office and they're very busy and the last thing they want to do is see a salesman. But if you see enough people each week you get clients. At the moment we're getting on average one client a day, though sometimes they use us only once. But if we continue to get one client a day, then after a year we should be fairly well established.'

John D says he has run up some appalling debts, 'which isn't surprising when I haven't had an income for ten months. But I have such confidence in this new firm that it is only a question of time before we start making some proper money.' After only a few weeks, Bow Street Runners is paying its way and giving him a small salary. Two previous problems, he felt, were his age and money. He is going to be twenty-one in a few weeks and says that he has grown out of feeling so ridiculously young . . . Money – well, 'this is the major difference between my old firm and my new firm. One of the biggest headaches with the old firm was the financial side of it. One had so much money owing and every week the wages had to be paid and, more often than not, there wasn't enough money in the bank account which meant that I had to go to the bank manager every four weeks. I don't have any of that now, being financed is a marvellous feeling. The main problem in this business is money and it's a problem I don't seem to have any more. Provided there's enough business done every week the money can be owing – because money can be siphoned out of the other firm.'

Apart from getting new clients, which will remain his key role, John D's main job at the moment is answering telephones, taking in jobs and giving them to riders. He keeps the books and does the invoicing every two weeks. Sooner or later the business will reach a size where he can employ somebody to answer the phone.

Another problem, also resolved, is his relationship with his partner. With Mark it wasn't easy to keep the situation on an even keel; as brothers they saw each other all the time, in work and outside. With Ken, his new partner, 'it's a healthy relationship simply because I don't know him that well; he comes to the office about once a week, we talk on the phone every day. It's a nice comforting feeling that he's been in the business seven to eight years. He knows what he's doing and basically he knows best, although he takes a lot of interest in what I say.'

Now that his first dispatch firm is history, John D sees it in a different light. 'I hadn't realized how much tension built up inside me, problem after problem, so many worries. Eighteen, which was the age I was, is basically too young to run a business. I made a lot of mistakes, learnt the hard way. I've learnt not to take people literally at their face value.' He still wants to make a fortune. In the meantime, 'the more I'm in business the more I seem to enjoy it, the more I'm learning, the more it fascinates me'.

Full-time
Capital: £1,500 for rent of offices, installation of telephones and advertising
Income: B (after a few weeks)

LETTING ROOMS

1976: Many people with a spare room or two would like to let it off and earn themselves some money into the bargain. It would be so easy, they muse, to put in a gas ring and turn the guest room into a bedsit and how nice it would be. Others, fingers burnt, swear never again or talk extensively about unpaid phone bills or yards of damp washing hanging in the bathroom. Everybody has a different recipe for successful landlord/tenant relations, but whatever is chosen must fit individual circumstances; there is no single well-tried formula.

First of all tenants, under the law, enjoy a good deal of protection: protection from eviction, harassment and excessive rents to name but three. A prospective landlord can find out his legal rights and duties from a solicitor or organization such as the Citizens Advice Bureau. Generally, the 'closer' you are to a tenant – in other words if you provide breakfast, clean the room and do the laundry – the more control you, as a landlord, retain. On the other hand, if you let out the self-contained basement flat, for example, your new tenant may seek a rent reduction from the Rent Tribunal and be difficult to move as well. Many people co-exist with a lodger or two for years at a time, but since this is an area fraught with legal niceties it is as well to know where you stand before you begin.

If you intend to let out a room or two in your own home, you have to decide exactly what kind of service you are going to provide and how much you are going to charge for it. Local experience is the best guide here. Judith R has let a couple of rooms to lodgers for several years and, on the whole, it has worked very well. Both rooms have wash-basins and kettles and one has a cooker. One tenant has just left after seven years. Judith R cleaned the room and washed the sheets, and it has been an ideal and undemanding relationship. The other room has been occupied by a series of tenants; the rent recently went up to £7.50 plus an evening's babysitting. Now that her own family is bursting at the seams one of the rooms is being brought back as a children's bedroom. The other room will probably be let to a 'house guest', who has the run of the place and basic food supplies such as tea, milk and bread. Looking at the house as a whole, Judith R has found it important to 'know I can go into all the rooms in the house. Otherwise it would just be a number of split-up units.'

That is one way of doing it. Fred M has an entirely different arrangement. He saved up enough money to buy an eight-roomed house on four floors in 1968 and, being single, intended to keep three rooms for himself, let out four separate rooms to four people and share a communal kitchen. He fixed the plumbing, put in a shower, gas fires in each room and a coin telephone on the landing. Then he advertised for tenants in *New Society*. 'Without vetting people,' he says, 'I arranged it so those people came who I wanted: ex-sociology students and social workers.' In his case the primary motive for letting rooms was not so much the rent as 'the difference between living on my own in a bedsit and being with people'. 'Being with people' means 'sharing a kitchen with me, the landlord. I made sure that I kept more territory than anyone else because they are transient and anyway it's my house.' For all its informality, Fred M's relations run smoothly with his tenants because, he suspects, both sides know what is expected of them. 'You have to know the limitations of the set-up,' he says, 'and you have to know what your real position is as a landlord. There's some flexibility but you can't demand too much.'

Despite his quip, 'I regard my tenants as walking pound notes,' Fred M charges well below market rents. 'In any case there is a wide band of market prices,' he says, 'depending on what is offered. I couldn't see myself living off rents because I wouldn't be prodded into doing anything.' Reasonable rents, he feels, are a key factor in peaceful relations. 'Rents are a heavy part of a person's income,' he says. 'If they are not a heavy part it makes a whole difference to the situation.' One side-effect of his renting policy is the reluctance of his tenants to leave. 'There are good reasons to leave after a while,' he says. 'People outgrow one room. I've got a feeling there are one or two dragging their heels about leaving and letting the money factor weigh too much.'

Seven months later: 'We've got no lodgers at the moment,' says Judith R. 'We've been decorating one of the rooms and in a couple of weeks the stair carpet will be down and then we'll see about it. I'm working in a playgroup four mornings a week and that gives me £14 a week clear.'

'My longest tenant has just left,' says Fred M, 'and I'm leaving the room empty for a bit while I see what happens. Apart from that, nothing new.'

Part-time
Capital: sufficient for the house in the first place
sufficient to equip room(s) with basic necessities such as heating and furniture (if provided)
no separate premises
Income: variable
Formal qualifications: none

1980: Fred M's last tenant moved four months ago, there is an inch of dust everywhere, and he is decorating the ground-floor rooms. 'I couldn't stand the inequality of the landlord/tenant relationship,' he says. 'You have to throw people out if you can't get on with them. I can't leave because this is my house.' But he admits he could be a landlord again, 'if circumstances changed or I needed the money. But at the moment I want a defined space that is my own. I don't want to hear everybody else rattling around in the kitchen.'

Judith R is letting her two spare rooms to foreign students studying English at summer school. They will be paying her £40 to £45 a week for accommodation, breakfast, evening meal and weekend meals.

'A neighbour was looking for places to stay for a batch of German schoolchildren and she asked me if I could help. They were seventeen to eighteen-year-olds, spoke very good English and we really enjoyed having them. Last summer I rang up the local school of English but there was nothing doing there. So I tried other schools and one of them put me on to a lady who is an agent. She deals with ten language schols, finding accommodation for students; she's very businesslike about it all and visits every household trying to ensure that students get matched with the right family. She wants to know what food we eat, what pets we have, if anyone in the house plays chess – that sort of thing.'

Part-time
Income: £40 to £45 a week per student, from which food, electricity, etc. must be deducted

ASTROLOGY
1976: Astrology is the study of celestial bodies, planets and stars and their effect on life on this earth, especially individual human life.

An astrologer's job is to construct and interpret horoscopes. It's a job which has been on the go for thousands of years and today's astrologers continue a long tradition.

Like many Geminis, so it is said, Martin F enjoys more than one occupation at any one time; as advertising manager for a large brewery he controls millions of pounds and as freelance astrologer he works in the evenings on individual horoscopes or on a book he is writing about the sun-sign Aquarius. An aunt originally interested him in astrology. 'She fed me information on anything weird you can think of,' he says; 'she even fed me books on flying saucers when I was in the airforce. When my daughter was born she said, "Oh, let me give her a birthday present of a horoscope," and that was fascinating. I had my chart done.'

Later on, Martin F went to astrology classes and took the Faculty of Astrological Studies correspondence course. Armed with a diploma in 1972, he was able to construct charts professionally. But there is a world of difference between knowing the basic information and being able to apply it, between the newspaper horoscopes, superficial and misleading as they are, and a recognition of astrology as a universal guide. 'Astrology can be used at many levels,' says Martin F, 'but I believe its most important use is as an aid to self-understanding and the need for people to understand the way they fit into the overall pattern. One likes to be able to point people in a direction which will help them grow, increase their awareness, their consciousness and assist in their search at whatever level that search is. The chart can be a very meaningful starting-off point.'

Martin F is personally interested in the movement of the planet from Pisces to Aquarius, in reincarnation and in Jungian analysis, which he is undergoing. Not all astrologers share the same beliefs. Some are quite happy to answer such questions as, 'When should I take my holidays?' Others specialize in predicting movements on the stock market, writing books or giving lectures and, of course, there is a gulf of expertise and experience between a £2 horoscope advertised in a magazine such as *Prediction* and a beautifully presented £40 chart. Martin F keeps his work simple and charges £8; he draws up a natal chart based on date, time and place of birth. 'They give me these details,' he says, 'and I try to find out why they want the chart done. They may say, "I'm having awful relationship problems," or "I don't know what to do about my career"; that's fine, one knows what to look for. Most people come to an astrologer at a point when, astrologically speaking, there's a lot happening: turbulence, change, depression, etc.'

Then, a few days later, astrologer and client meet for a couple of hours in the evening. They discuss the chart and all its implications. Martin F does not give a written analysis. 'It is nice to have something written that you can refer to from time to time,' he says, 'but my typing is bad and slow and most people seem quite happy to bring along a tape recorder or they take notes.' These sessions are essential for him, he says, because 'this is where you learn and develop as an astrologer, by having people sitting down with you, telling you their problems and you trying to help them.' It is not work to undertake lightly, bordering as it does on medicine and therapy, and it is probably not full-time work either, except for a few well-established astrologers. At any rate, Martin F is staying in his job for the time being.

Eight months later: 'I finished the book on time and it's being published in Italy, but goodness knows how the money is going to get out of the country, there's such financial chaos. I've recently cut down my work with the Astrological Association, though I still teach one evening a week at the Faculty of Astrological Studies. I'm also taking two evenings for group therapy which I think will help with the consultations.'

Part-time
Capital: none
  no separate premises
Income: A
Formal qualifications: Diploma of the Faculty of Astrological Studies

1980: Last year Martin F gave up his well-paid advertising job and set himself up as a counsellor and astrological consultant. Working from the basement of a bookshop, he constructs natal charts and also sees people for counselling: businessmen, housewives, retired drug addicts – anyone who feels himself to be in a crisis. The Chinese character for 'crisis' is the same as that for 'opportunity', he says. 'There are perhaps three kinds of people wanting counselling'; the seriously disturbed, the averagely distressed and the searchers. The people in the middle group will either gravitate towards the searchers and have, if you like, a crisis of meaning and wonder what it's all about or they'll have a crisis crisis and realize they've got to seek some help.'

Giving advice over the garden fence is one thing, but setting up as a professional counsellor requires care and patience and some knowledge of oneself. Martin F is studying for his master's degree before training to be a Jungian analytical psychologist. As necessary work for that training, he is undergoing two or three hours a week of personal analysis. 'You have to go through the process yourself and find out who you are. Having found out who you are you learn not to mind and then you are in a position to re-evaluate whether you still want to be an analyst.'

Counselling is not work to be taken on lightly. 'The things that are not fully conscious in ourselves we tend to see in other people . . . it may well be something within ourselves that we haven't worked out. In the therapeutic situation, the therapist has to handle projections from the client and also be balanced enough himself to handle any projections he may himself hold. An unconscious power drive can be particularly dangerous – many "helpers", from analysts to social workers and even vicars, are sometimes trying to exert power over people without realizing it.'

Having said that, there is a clear need for counsellors. Martin F usually sees his clients once a week: 'The thing I like about the work, whether it is first-aid counselling or on-going counselling or astrological charts, is not to fit the person into any water-tight compartment or mould, but to try and help that person find out who they really are so they can live naturally without the conditioning of parents, family, school. For example, a man may be expected to be a steely-eyed executive. He might be better off doing a completely different kind of job. My own story perhaps. I see myself as a guide going with a person on their personal journey and helping them to help themselves so that at some point they're going to feel strong enough to stand on their own two feet and not to need the therapist.'

Does he miss his advertising job?

'Not nearly as much as I thought I was going to. I don't know whether my analysis is working or whether I am much more at peace with myself, but the financial side, which is uncertain to say the least, I don't find nearly as worrying as I might have done.' With a wife and child to support, Martin F wants a good income; unemployment benefit when he first left his job and redundancy money eased the changeover and he expects, in time, to be earning well. 'I find that I'm busy but I'm conscious of the fact that I'm only earning when I'm working and that when I'm working I've got to be working well. I do often feel the pressure when working on a chart – ''This is all time and money'' – whereas in a salaried job you can have an off day, you can sit back.'

Full-time
Capital: none
Income: £30 for chart plus year's trends (five to six hours work)
  counselling according to what people can pay; about £5 to £10 an hour
Formal qualifications: counselling course
  Diploma of the Faculty of Astrological Studies
  Martin F is also hoping to train with the Association of Jungian Analysts
Experience: group therapy

APPENDIX

The following sections were compiled with the assistance of Anne Montague of the *Observer* Careers Service.

Many of the self-employed, including some in this book, start in a small way: developing a hobby or expanding a second line of work. Others have low overheads and cannot fall very far. Still more find that their business requires considerable investment and corresponding commitment. Whatever your situation the following checklists, names and addresses should prove useful.

FACTS AND FIGURES

Anybody can work for themselves – there are no limits of age, race, gender or occupation. You may want to exploit a redundancy payment, get out of a run-of-the-mill job, be financially independent or develop a new technology or idea. But before you hand in your notice ask yourself the following questions:

Skills

Identify your personal skills. Are they administrative or technical? Ideally they should be both. What other skills do you have? If you intend to work for yourself you will need to have a balanced range of skills at your fingertips. Mark down any which you do not have and consider taking a partner.

Motivation

How much do you want to work for yourself? A 'wait and see' attitude will only suffice if your commitment is small and you can afford to be flexible. Those, however, who put their eggs in one basket must be prepared to work hard and enlist the full co-operation of their families in the venture.

Ideas

The world is full of people with 'good ideas' – *but*, can you identify a need for your product/service? Will people be willing to pay money to satisfy that need? Investigate the market – talk to people in the business, identify your potential competitors.

Finance

The amount of money you need can be calculated by combining the following sets of information:

i) the number of products you can sell in a given market at various prices
ii) the cost of producing different numbers of the product/service and selling them in the market. Costs include overheads such as rent, heating, lighting, telephone

The cheapest money available, even at high interest rates, is an overdraft from the bank. Banks and other financial institutions, however, are wary of lending to new companies who have not yet proved themselves. You are likely to have to find a substantial amount of initial capital from your own resources in the form of:

i) cash
ii) assets which can be realized, eg a car which can be sold
iii) assets which can be pledged as security, eg a house (though be wary of promising the roof over your head)

When setting up on your own you can operate in a number of different ways:

Sole tradership

You work on your own as a private person, take the profits and are liable for the business. If the business fails your personal possessions can be sold to pay the debts.

Partnership

The same as sole tradership but two or more people (up to twenty) share the responsibilities. Each partner is equally responsible for debts and liabilities.

Limited liability company

The company is a separate legal entity that can sue and be sued. The owners of the company are responsible for the company debts only to the extent of the face value of the shares in the company issued to them – and not to the extent of their personal possessions.

What else do you have to consider?

Location

Location may or may not be critical – it depends on what you are trying to sell and where your 'raw materials' come from. Generally it makes sense to be located near your customers and suppliers of raw materials.

Timing

Timing may be all-important. Examine your market – is it likely to be subject to seasonal fluctuations? Starting business in a low season may allow you time to consolidate before demand builds up. Is your product fashionable? Are your raw materials likely to cost you a good deal more in the near future?

Financial planning

Under-capitalization is the major cause of failure in small businesses. Apart from initial capital you will need to finance the growth of the business until profits start to return capital investment. Use a good accountant and be wary of borrowing too much at the start of a business.

Marketing

Marketing means looking at the product/service from the customer's point of view. Identify your potential customers – how does your product/service satisfy their needs? What proportion of the market are you likely to obtain? Compare your product/service with those of your competitors, in terms of price and design.

Official permission

Local and national planning regulations specify the type of business that can be set up in specific areas. Almost any building alterations require planning permission – check with the local authority and in any property lease you intend to buy.

Insurance

You should be insured against claims on your business by third parties for negligence and faulty goods/services as well as against fire and theft.

COURSES

Polytechnics, technical colleges, colleges of further education and management centres throughout the country run courses in business studies, many with particular reference to small business. Contact local or regional advisory council, education authority or public library.

Various organizations and institutions run one-day or weekend seminars and training courses, eg Chambers of Commerce and Industry, National Federation of Self-Employed & Small Businesses Ltd (see page 191–2).

Manpower Services Commission

Funds training courses under the Training Opportunities Scheme (TOPS) for people wanting to set up their own business. New Enterprise Programmes (NEPs) are held at Manchester, Durham, London and Glasgow Business Schools. Small Business Courses (SBCs) are held at Management Centres throughout the country. Courses are advertised in the press. Contact District or Regional Office of the Manpower Services Commission's Training Services Division.

City University Business School, London

Programmes of courses on starting a new business, run by URBED (Urban & Economic Development) Ltd in association with the Training Services Division and the London Enterprise Programme. Contact Course Co-ordinator, URBED, 359 The Strand, London WC2R 0HP. Tel. 01-379 7525.

Thames Polytechnic

One-day workshops on starting a business. Contact School of Business Administration, Thames Polytechnic, Riverside House Annexe, Reresford St, Woolwich, London SE18 6BU. Tel. 01-854 2030.

London Enterprise Programme

Programmes on starting a business are run by the London Enterprise Agency in conjunction with the GLC at the Polytechnic of Central London. Contact LEntA, London Chamber of Commerce & Industry, 69 Cannon St, London EC4N 5AB. Tel. 01-236 2676/7.

National Extension College

Arranges evening classes in the south-west in conjunction with the adult-education services. Offers advice, information and support for people starting up. 46a Fore St, Ivybridge PL21 9AE. Tel. Ivybridge 3949.

National Institute of Adult Education

Publishes *Year Book of Adult Education* and *Residential Short Courses.* From National Institute of Adult Education, 19b De Montfort St, Leicester LE1 7GE. Price £2.75 and 75p respectively.

Management Education and Development for Small Businesses

A comprehensive survey of the educational provision for small businesses throughout the country. Prepared for the Foundation for Management Education it describes all centres, including industrial training boards, independent and other organizations. Obtainable on request from Dr R. D. Bennett, Thames Valley Regional Management Centre, Wellington St, Slough S11 1YG.

FINANCING THE BUSINESS

All the clearing banks make provision for assisting new business ventures. Free booklets, on assistance with business finance, can be obtained from all branches of the banks. The Midland and Lloyds are particularly active in this field.

Development Capital Ltd

Loans from £75,000 upwards. 88 Baker St, London W1 Tel. 01-486 5021

Industrial and Commercial Finance Corporation Ltd

Long-term finance from £5,000 to £2 million. 91 Waterloo Rd, London SE1 8XP Tel. 01-928 7822

National Research Development Corporation

Finance for development of new products and processes and licences companies to manufacture new products based on research in universities or Government laboratories. Kingsgate House, 66–74 Victoria St, London SW1E 6SL Tel. 01-828 3400

Rainford Venture Capital

Equity capital between £50,000 to £300,000 available to entrepreneurs who can expect to achieve a turnover of over £1 million within three to four years and are prepared to set up in business within the metropolitan borough of St Helens. The Rainford Venture Capital, Rainford Hall, Crank Rd, Crank, St Helens, Merseyside WA11 7RP Tel. St Helens 0744 37227

INFORMATION AND ADVICE

Small Firms Service

This comprises eleven centres, operated by the Small Firms Division of the Department of Industry, offering information, sign-posting, counselling and free booklets on running a business (see page 195). In cases of difficulty contact Small Firms Division, Abell House, John Islip St, London SW1P 4LN Tel. 01-211 5245.

North: 22 Newgate Shopping Centre
Newcastle upon Tyne NE1 5RH
Tel. Newcastle 25353; Freefone 529

North-west: Peter House, Oxford St
Manchester M1 5AN
Tel. Manchester 832 5282; Freefone 6005

Liverpool: 1 Old Hall St
Liverpool L3 9HJ
Tel. Liverpool 236 5756; Freefone 6005

Yorkshire & Humberside: 1 Park Row, City Sq
Leeds LS1 5NR
Tel. Leeds 445151; Freefone 5361

East Midlands: 48–50 Maid Marian Way
Nottingham NG1 6GF
Tel. Nottingham 49791; Freefone 4062

West Midlands: 53 Stephenson St
Birmingham B2 4DH
Tel. Birmingham 643 3344; Freefone 4054

East: 35 Wellington St
Luton LU1 2SB
Tel. Luton 29215; Freefone 372

London & south-east: 65 Buckingham Palace Rd
London SW1W 0QX
Tel. 01-828 2384; Freefone 2079

South-west: Colston Centre, Colston Ave
Bristol BS1 4UB
Tel. Bristol 294546; Freefone 9910

Scotland: 57 Bothwell St
Glasgow G2 6TU
Tel. Glasgow 248 6014; Freefone 846

Wales: 16 St David's House, Wood St
Cardiff CF1 1ER
Tel. Cardiff 396116; Freefone 1208

Industrial Development Associations

North of England Development Council: Sank House, Carliol Sq, Newcastle-upon-Tyne NE1 6XE
Tel. Newcastle 610026

North West Industrial Development Association: Brazennose House, Brazennose St, Manchester M2 5AZ
Tel. Manchester 834 6778

Yorkshire & Humberside Development Association: Civic Hall, Leeds LS1 3AZ
Tel. Leeds 444639

Wales

WELSH DEVELOPMENT AGENCY
The Small Business Unit offers advisory service, guidance and training in a range of business functions and craft skills. Loans.
Head office: Treforest Industrial Estate, Pontypridd, Glamorgan CF37 5UT Tel. Treforest 2666
Local offices: 'Isnant', Glynne Rd, Bangor, Gwynedd Tel. Gwynedd 52606/7/8
Ladywell House, Newtown, Powys Tel. Newtown 27333
7 Nevill St, Abergavenny, Gwent Tel. Abergavenny 5588
Wrexham Industrial Estate, Wrexham, Clwyd Tel. Wrexham 61621
37 King St, Carmarthen, Dyfed Tel. Carmarthen 5642/6689
Swansea Industrial Estate, Swansea, Glamorgan Tel. Swansea 32821/33850

DEVELOPMENT BOARD FOR RURAL WALES
Help for small businesses in mid-Wales. Advisory service. Loans. Factories and workshops. NEP courses. Marketing Director, Ladywell House, Newtown, Powys SY16 1JB Tel. Newtown 26965

NORTH WALES EMPLOYMENT RESOURCE & ADVICE CENTRE
Advises people already in business. Assists redundant workers; encourages village co-operatives. Bradford House, Denbigh St, Llanrwst, Gwynedd Tel. Llanrwst 641280

Scotland

SCOTTISH DEVELOPMENT AGENCY
The Small Business Division offers professional advice and technical instruction. Loans and other capital. Small factories and workshops. 101 Telford Rd, Edinburgh EH4 2NP Tel. Edinburgh 343 1911/6

HIGHLANDS & ISLANDS DEVELOPMENT BOARD
Helps finance business ventures through grants, low-interest loans, minority shareholding. Factories and workshops available. Advisory and support service. Director of Industrial Development & Marketing, Bridge House, 27 Bank St, Inverness IV1 1QR Tel. Inverness 34171

Northern Ireland

NORTHERN IRELAND DEVELOPMENT AGENCY
Help for new manufacturing enterprises. Guidance on financial incentives offered by Department of Commerce. Assistance with start-up capital and expansion. 'Maryfield', 100 Belfast Rd, Holywood, Co. Down BT18 9QX Tel. Holywood 4232

LOCAL ENTERPRISE DEVELOPMENT UNIT (LEDU)
Promotes manufacturing and service industries. Advisory service. Grants and loans. Government sites and factories made available. Assistance for craftwork. Lamond House, Purdy's Lane, Newtownbreda, Belfast BT8 4TB Tel. Belfast 691031

Local Authorities

Many local authorities – county, district, town and borough councils – offer help and advice to small firms. Contact Industrial or Economic Development Officer at County or Town Hall. Information often available from local library.

Three specific examples:

BARNSLEY METROPOLITAN BOROUGH COUNCIL
Nursery factories. Property register. Loans and grants in addition to regional development grants. Michael Wedgeworth, Industrial Development Centre, 8 Eastgate, Barnsley, Yorkshire Tel. Barnsley 88489

MERSEYSIDE COUNTY COUNCIL

Merseyside County Economic Development Office (MERCEDO) offers county grants in addition to government grants in specified areas for both manufacturing and service industries. Advice and counselling. Jack Miller, Tithebarn House, Tithebarn St, Liverpool L2 2PH Tel. Liverpool 227 5234

NORTHUMBERLAND COUNTY COUNCIL

Information and advice. Small Business Grant Scheme in addition to Government incentives for remoter rural areas. Workshop units available. Industrial/Development Officer, Northumberland County Council, County Hall, Newcastle-upon-Tyne NE1 1SA Tel. Newcastle 26613/24180/23940

Other National Organizations

ACTION RESOURCES CENTRE

Acts as broker in matching secondees from business and industry to long-term community projects and small enterprises. Helps with particular skills. For information on types of projects considered and nearest regional/area manager send s.a.e. to Central Office, 4 Cromwell Place, London SW7 2JJ Tel. 01-584 0438

BRITISH STEEL CORPORATION (INDUSTRY) LTD

Offers help and incentives to new industry in areas where BSC modernization is causing unemployment. Incentives in addition to Government grants and loans in Special Development and Development Areas. BSC (Industry) Ltd, 42 Grosvenor Gardens, London SW1W 0EB Tel. 01-235 1212

The following BSC (Industry) Ltd Small Business Developments offer purpose-built factory space/workshop units and counselling for tenants:

Cardiff Workshops Ltd, BSC (Industry) Ltd, Gabalfa, Cardiff CF4 1XS Tel. Cardiff 62161

Tollcross Industrial Village, Fullarton Rd, Tollcross, Glasgow G32 8YL Tel. Glasgow 641 4972

Glengarnock Industrial Development Ltd, BSC (Industry) Ltd, Glengarnock Task Force, Walker Memorial Hall, Main St, Kilbirnie, Ayreshire KA25 7BX Tel. Kilbirnie 5455

Hartlepool Workshops Ltd, BSC Hartlepool Works, PO Box 20, Hartlepool, Cleveland TS25 2EF Tel. Hartlepool 66611

COUNCIL FOR SMALL INDUSTRIES IN RURAL AREAS (CoSIRA)

Advice and counselling for small businesses in the English rural areas.

Loans and help with premises. Training workshops in skills and crafts. Head office will advise on nearest local organizer. Queen's House, Fish Row, Salisbury, Wiltshire SP1 1EX Tel. Salisbury 24411

CRAFTS COUNCIL

Promotes Britain's artist-craftsmen. Offers range of schemes including workshop training, 'new craftsmen' grants, loans and bursaries. 8 Waterloo Place, London SW1Y 4AU Tel. 01-839 6309

Local Organizations

COMMUNITY OF ST HELENS TRUST LTD

Advice and assistance, including premises and finance for business ventures in the district. Help with opportunities and training. Loans when essential. PO Box 36, St Helens, Merseyside Tel. St Helens 28882, ex. 2570/2568/1652

DARTINGTON NORTH DEVON TRUST

Aims to promote and establish small businesses and work opportunities for people living in North Devon or intending to work in the area. Small factory units, carp farming, small-scale agricultural engineering, community service scheme and other projects. Bridge Chambers, Barnstaple, North Devon EX31 1HB Tel. Barnstaple 76324

ICI MOND DIVISION

Advice on setting up a small firm, on financial and technical problems. Help with premises. Castner Kellner Works, Runcorn, Cheshire WA4 JE Tel. Runcorn 73434

ENTERPRISE LANCASTER

Advice for smaller firms in the area. Information on industrial sites and buildings. Low rental start-up accommodation. Small Firms Club. R. H. Kelsall, Town Hall, Lancaster LA 1PH. Tel. Lancaster 65272

ENTERPRISE NORTH

Advice and guidance to people wishing to start small businesses in the north of England. A free, voluntary organization. Derek Craven, Co-ordinator & Liaison Officer, Durham University Business School, Mill Hill Lane, Durham DH1 3LB Tel. Durham 41919

LEICESTERSHIRE SMALL FIRMS CENTRE

Helps small firms with advice and counselling, management consultancy and project teams. Seminars and courses. Help with property and planning. 8 St Martins, Leicester LE1 5DD Tel. Leicester 22632

MENDIP & WANSDYKE LOCAL ENTERPRISE GROUP
Information and advice on any aspect of setting up a business. Help with premises and planning. Roger Kelly, Ammerdown, Radstock, Bath BA3 5SW Tel. Radstock 35321/33809

PENNINE DEVELOPMENT TRUST
Renovates and converts old buildings in the Pennines to provide small workshop accommodation. Business information and advice to people setting up in the area. The Birchcliffe Centre, Hebden Bridge, West Yorkshire HX7 8DG Tel. Hebden Bridge 3626

WEST SOMERSET SMALL INDUSTRIES GROUP
Liaises between small firms and local councils. Advice on starting up and information on premises. 29 Swain St, Watchet, Somerset TA23 0AD Tel. Watchet 31277

London

BARLEY MOW WORKSPACE
Factory converted into community of small businesses. Shared facilities provide wide range of services. 10 Barley Mow Passage, Chiswick, London W4 4PH Tel. 01-994 6477

CLERKENWELL WORKSHOPS
Self-contained workshop units at low inclusive rentals. Loan facilities. Business counselling by City University. 31 Clerkenwell Close, London EC1 Tel. 01-251 3273

HACKNEY BUSINESS PROMOTION CENTRE
Help with business projects, management, training, premises. Counselling on all aspects of business, including finance. 1–11 Hoxton St, London N1 4NL Tel. 01-739 9606

ISLINGTON SMALL BUSINESS COUNSELLING SERVICE
Established by the Action Resource Centre. Gives advice to any business operating, or intending to operate, in the area. 201–2 Upper St, London N1 1RQ Tel. 01-359 3924

LADY MARGARET HALL SETTLEMENT
Through Employment Development Officer provides support in establishing small businesses in Lambeth, particularly co-operatives. 131 Kennington Rd, London SE11 6SN Tel. 01-735 1024/5035

LAMBETH INDUSTRIES
Low-cost flexible space for new or developing business. Shared facilities and services. Free management and technical consultancy

through link with London Enterprise Agency. John Hughes, Locks D & E, Parkhall Trading Estate, Martell Rd, London SE21 Tel. 01-761 3600/735 1024

LONDON ENTERPRISE AGENCY (LEntA)

Help and advice on all business problems. In conjunction with London Industrial Centre runs 'London Enterprise Programme' for people starting a business at Polytechnic of Central London. Organizes exhibitions. LEntA, London Chamber of Commerce and Industry, 69 Cannon St, London EC4N 5AB Tel. 01-236 2676/7

LONDON INDUSTRIAL CENTRE – GLC

Advice and counselling to small firms and new start-ups. Help with premises, planning and other statutory requirements. Sources of finance. Industrial expansion and housing for key workers. Island Block, County Hall, London SE1 7PB Tel. 01-633 7494

TOWER HAMLETS CENTRE FOR SMALL BUSINESS

Advice and counselling for local small firms and new start-ups on all business problems. Guidance on finding premises and raising finance. Training courses and seminars. 17 Whitechurch Lane, London E1 7QR Tel. 01-247 8846

URBED (ECONOMIC & URBAN DEVELOPMENT) LTD

Non-profit-making research and consultancy group offering advice on potential re-use of empty buildings or waste land by small firms in urban areas. Runs courses (London only) on starting a business. 359 The Strand, London WC2R 0HP Tel. 01-379 7525

Local Small Business Clubs

TEESSIDE SMALL BUSINESS CLUB

Aims to further interests of small businesses in Cleveland and surrounding areas by representation, exchange of ideas, promotion, advice and support. 92 Grange Rd, Middlesbrough, Cleveland TS1 2LS Tel. Middlesbrough 217802

Similar groups include:

BRIDGETOWN BUSINESS CLUB, Mr W. Hibberd, Milroy Engineering Co. Ltd, 23 McPhail St, Glasgow G40 1EL Tel. Glasgow 554 2344

DURHAM ASSOCIATION FOR BUSINESS, INDUSTRY AND COMMERCE, Ian Thorpe, New College Durham, Framwellgate Moor Centre, Durham Tel. Durham 62421

KIDDERMINSTER SMALL FIRMS DISCUSSION GROUP, Mr P. Ingham, Dept. of Carpet Technology, Textiles & Management, Kidderminster College, Hoo Rd, Kidderminster, Worcestershire DY10 1LX Tel. Kidderminster 66311/2/3/4

LANCASTER SMALL FIRMS CLUB, Enterprise Lancaster, Town Hall, Lancaster LA1 1PH Tel. Lancaster 65272

LEEDS SMALL BUSINESS ASSOCIATION, Peter Daniels, Unit U, Canal Basin, Neville St, Leeds 1 Tel. Leeds 440804

TYNE & WEAR SMALL BUSINESS CLUB, John Parkes, 2 Lyndon Grove, East Boldon, Tyne & Wear Tel. Sunderland 362553

New Town Development Corporations

Contact Managing Director of each corporation for information on provision of premises and other assistance for small businesses:

Acycliffe
Basildon
Bracknell
Central Lancashire
Corby
Cumbernauld
Dwmbran
East Kilbride
Glenrothes
Harlow
Irwine
Livingston
Mid-Wales (Newtown)
Milton Keynes
Northampton
Peterborough
Peterlee
Redditch
Runcorn
Skelmersdale
Stevenage
Telford
Warrington
Washington

Co-operatives

CO-OPERATIVE DEVELOPMENT AGENCY

Represents and promotes the co-operative movement. Advice on how to form, manage and finance a co-operative. 20 Albert Embankment, London SE1 7TJ Tel. 01-211 4633

INDUSTRIAL COMMON OWNERSHIP MOVEMENT (ICOM)

Help and advice on common-ownership co-operatives. Training course on how to run small-scale co-operatives. Loans available through Industrial Common Ownership Finance Ltd, Beechwood College, Elmete Lane, Rounday, Leeds LS8 2LQ Tel. Leeds 651235

SCOTTISH CO-OPERATIVES DEVELOPMENT COMMITTEE
Information and advice for existing and potential workers' co-operatives throughout Scotland. Through its Development Project is seeking to initiate new co-operatives in Clydeside. Cairns Campbell, Development Officer, 120 Morrison St, Glasgow G5 8LP Tel. Glasgow 429 1488

Shared Workshop Premises
Comprehensive lists of premises offering workshop space and shared facilities for small businesses were published in *The Architects Journal* under the series title: 'Use of Redundant Buildings for Small Businesses':
i. Working communities in the London area – Dec. 6 1978 (Vol. 168 No 4)
ii. Conversion projects throughout the UK – Aug. 22 1979 (Vol. 170 No 3)

Membership Organizations
ASSOCIATION OF BRITISH CHAMBERS OF COMMERCE
Chambers of Commerce and Industry throughout the country provide a wide range of services for small firms, including advice and information on business problems, training courses, seminars and workshops. Membership: manufacturing, commercial and professional firms. 6–14 Dean Farrar St, London SW1X 0DX Tel. 01-222 0201
NATIONAL CHAMBER OF TRADE
Information and advice on setting up in service industries and retail trades direct from own resources or through associated specialist trade and professional bodies. Enterprise House, Henley-on-Thames, Oxon RG9 1TU Tel. Henley 6161
CONFEDERATION OF BRITISH INDUSTRY (CBI)
Principal representative body for industry and commerce. High proportion of members are small firms, represented through its Smaller Firms Council. 21 Tothill St, London SW1H 9LP Tel. 01-930 6711
ALLIANCE OF SMALL FIRMS & SELF-EMPLOYED PEOPLE LTD
Advisory service and legal-aid schemes. 279 Church Rd, London SE19 2QQ Tel. 653 7288/4576
ASSOCIATION OF INDEPENDENT BUSINESSES
Information and advisory service, specializing in industrial relations problems, finance and commercial legislation. Assists new business

by providing contact with others. Trowbray House, 108 Weston St, London SE1 3QB Tel. 01-403 4066

INSTITUTE OF SMALL BUSINESS

Publishes quarterly newsletter. Free written advisory service to subscribers. Seminars, mail forwarding and telephone-message service. Tower Suite, 1 Whitehall Place, London SW1A 2HQ Tel. 01-930 5577

NATIONAL FEDERATION OF SELF-EMPLOYED & SMALL BUSINESSES LTD

Local branches throughout the country offer counselling and advice for people starting up. One-day courses. Free booklet: *Be Your Own Boss – how to become self-employed*. 32 St Annes Rd West, St Annes-on-Sea, Lancashire FY8 1NY Tel. St Annes 720911

SPECIALIZED INFORMATION

This information is arranged according to the chapter in which the relevant occupations were discussed.

ONE: MINISTRY OF AGRICULTURE, FISHERIES AND FOOD (PUBLICATIONS)

Publishes books, maps and leaflets on any crop. Also *At the Farmer's Service*, a reference booklet on government services such as grants (from HMSO). Tolcarne Drive, Pinner, Middlesex

AGRICULTURAL DEVELOPMENT AND ADVISORY SERVICE

Advisory service. Regional offices give free technical and scientific advice. Gt Westminster House, Horseferry Rd, London SW1 Tel. 01-216 6681

AGRICULTURAL TRAINING BOARD

Leaflets on careers. 32–4 Beckenham Rd, Beckenham, Kent Tel. 01-650 4890

ROYAL HORTICULTURAL SOCIETY

Horticultural Hall, Vincent Sq, London SW1 Tel. 01-834 4333

SOIL ASSOCIATION

Organic farming and gardening. Review, books, pamphlets, courses. Walnut Tree Manor, Haughley, Stowmarket, Suffolk Tel. Haughley 235

HENRY DOUBLEDAY RESEARCH ASSOCIATION

Organic association. Publications, seeds, organic pesticides. 32 Convent Lane, Bocking, Braintree, Essex Tel. Braintree 24083

ORGANIC FARMERS AND GROWERS LTD
Co-operative for marketing produce of farmers using biological methods. 5 Station Rd, Stowmarket, Suffolk Tel. Stowmarket 2315
THE BRITISH BEE-KEEPERS' ASSOCIATION
High Trees, Dean Lane, Worstham, Surrey Tel. Downland 53111
THE BRITISH HORSE SOCIETY
Advice on training for a career with horses. Examinations and tests. British Equestrian Centre, Stoneleigh, Kenilworth, Warwickshire Tel. Coventry 52241
PONIES OF BRITAIN
To promote the well-being of ponies. Information sheets on riding stables, trekking centres, care of ponies. Ascot Racecourse, Ascot, Berkshire. Tel. Winkfield Row 2508

TWO: SOCIETY OF INDUSTRIAL ARTISTS AND DESIGNERS
To promote high standards of design for the benefit of the public, industry and commerce. *Designer*, monthly, 12 Carlton House Terrace, London SW1 Tel. 01-930 1911
THE DESIGN COUNCIL
Displays, exhibitions, competitions. *Design* monthly. Also Design Council in Cardiff and Glasgow. 28 Haymarket, London SW1 Tel. 01-839 8000
INSTITUTE OF LINGUISTS
Professional organization for technical and commercial linguists. Conferences, insurance, information service. 24a Highbury Grove, London N5 Tel. 01-359 7445
THE TRANSLATORS ASSOCIATION
Literary translating. Members must have at least one work published in UK. 84 Drayton Gardens, London SW10 Tel. 01-373 6642
THE BRITISH COMPUTER SOCIETY
Learned and professional society for computing practitioners. Regional branches. 13 Mansfield St, London W1 Tel. 01-637 0471
THE MARKET RESEARCH SOCIETY
Professional body. Sends out lists of organizations which employ interviewers. 15 Belgrave Sq, London W1 Tel. 01-235 4709
ASSOCIATION OF MARKET SURVEY ORGANIZATIONS
Trade association. Lists organizations which employ interviewers. RBL, PO Box 203, Green Bank, London E19 PA Tel. 01-488 1366

THREE: DISTRIBUTIVE INDUSTRY TRAINING BOARD
Publishes *Mind Your Own Business* for small shopkeepers and other

booklets on various sections of the retail trade. Maclaren House, Talbot Rd, Stretford, Manchester Tel. Manchester 872 2494

THE BOOKSELLERS' ASSOCIATION
Professional association. 154 Buckingham Palace Rd, London SW1 Tel. 01-730 8214

PROVINCIAL BOOKSELLERS' FAIRS ASSOCIATION
Antiquarian and second-hand booksellers. 3 Crescent Rd, Worthing, Sussex Tel. Worthing 31169

THE ASSOCIATION OF ILLUSTRATORS
Bimonthly magazine. 17 Carlton House Terrace, London SW1 Tel. 01-930 5071/6056

NATIONAL MARKET TRADERS' FEDERATION
Yorkshire Bank Chambers, Loundside, Chapeltown, Yorkshire Tel. Ecclesfield 65395

FOUR: THE BUILDING CENTRE
Regional centres. Information and displays of building products and materials. 26 Store St, London WC1 Tel. 01-637 8361

FIVE: THE BRITISH ASSOCIATION FOR EARLY CHILDHOOD EDUCATION
Concerned with children's education from birth to about eight years. Montgomery Hall, Kennington Oval, London SE11 Tel. 01-582 8744

THE MONTESSORI SOCIETY AMI(UK)
Aims to propagate the Montessori method of education and the principles for which it stands. Leaflets, books, magazine. 26 Lyndhurst Gardens, London NW3 Tel. 01-435 7874

SIX: For information on crafts see *Crafts Council* (page 187) and CoSIRA (page 186)

SEVEN: THE BREWERS' SOCIETY
Provides information on running a pub and how to apply. Organizes and runs residential training schemes. 42 Portman Sq, London W1 Tel. 01-486 4831

THE CORDON BLEU COOKERY SCHOOL
114 Marylebone Lane, London W1 Tel. 01-935 3503

PUPPET CENTRE TRUST
Theatre, workshops, information, library. Battersea Arts Centre, Lavender Hill, London SW11 Tel. 01-228 5335

EIGHT: THE NATIONAL CHILDBIRTH TRUST
Provides information on childbirth, especially natural methods. 9 Queensborough Terrace, London W2 Tel. 01-229 9319

CENTRAL MIDWIVES BOARD
For information on training. 39 Harrington Gardens, London SW7 Tel. 01-373 4801

ENGLISH TOURIST BOARD
Thirteen regional boards. Promotes the tourist industry. 4 Grosvenor Gardens, London SW1 Tel. 01-730 3400

LONDON TOURIST BOARD
Promotes tourism in London. 26 Grosvenor Gardens, London SW1 Tel. 01-730 3450

THE COLLEGE OF TRADITIONAL CHINESE ACUPUNCTURE
Trains acupuncturists. Tao House, Queensway, Leamington Spa, Warwickshire Tel. Leamington Spa 39347

INTERNATIONAL COLLEGE OF ORIENTAL MEDICINE
Trains acupuncturists. East Grinstead, Sussex Tel. East Grinstead 26567

FACULTY OF ASTROLOGICAL STUDIES
Correspondence course and classes in London. Hook Cottage, Vines Cross, Heathfield, Sussex

ASTROLOGICAL ASSOCIATION
Lectures, meetings, conferences. 36 Tweedie Rd, Bromley, Kent

BIBLIOGRAPHY

Starting a Retail Business, *Raising Finance for New Enterprises*, *Obtaining a Franchise*, *Marketing*, *Starting in Business*, *Finding Commercial Information* and several others from the Small Firms Service. Available, free, from their information centres (see page 183).

Starting in Business and *Employers Guide to PAYE* (P7) (Inland Revenue). Available from local branches.

Should I be Registered for VAT (Customs and Excise). Available from local offices.

Small Firms Employment Subsidy and *The Rights of Employees – a Guide for Employers* (Department of Employment). Available from Job Centres and Employment Offices.

Money for Business and *Money for Export* (Bank of England, 1978). From Industrial Finance Unit of Economic and Intelligence Department, Bank of England, London EC2R 8AH. Price £1 and £1.25 respectively, including p. & p.

The Small Business Kit (National Extension College). How to assess business ideas, raise money, find premises, sell product/service, control finances, start a co-operative. From National Extension College, 18 Brookland Avenue, Cambridge CB2 2HN. Price £4.55 plus 60p p. & p.

Know Your Business (British Institute of Management, 1978). From Publication Sales, BIM, Management House, Parker St, London WC2B 5PT. Price £6 for members; £9 for non-members including p. & p.

The Pitfalls of Managing a Small Business – and How to Avoid Them. Free from Dun & Bradstreet Ltd, PO Box 17, 26 Clifton St, London EC2P 2LY.

The Complete Guide to Managing Your Business (Eaglemoss, 1980). Updated bi-monthly. From Managing Your Business Ltd, 87 Elystan St, London SW3 6RL. Price £39.50 including p. & p.

Financial Management Handbook (Kluwer). Updated three times a year. From Kluwer Publishing Ltd, 1 Harlequin Avenue, Great West Rd, Brentford, Mddx TW8 9EW. Price £55 (1981) plus £2.50 p. & p.

Earning Money at Home (Consumers Association). From Consumers Association, Caxton Hill, Hertford SG13 7LZ. Price £3.95 including p. & p.

Croner's Reference Book for the Self-Employed and Smaller Business (Croner). Updated monthly. From Croner Publications Ltd, Croner House, 173 Kingston Rd, New Malden, Surrey KT3 4QL. Price £18 including p. & p.

Export Handbook (British Overseas Trade Board). From Export Services Division, Export House, 50 Ludgate Hill, London EC4N 7HU. Price £2.50 including p. & p.

Rural Resettlement Handbook (Rural Resettlement Group, 1979). From Rural Resettlement Group, Manor House, Thelnetham, Diss, Norfolk. Price £1.80 post free.

The Financing of Small Businesses, J. Bates (Sweet & Maxwell, London 1971).

Small Businesses, P. Clarke (David & Charles, Newton Abbot, 1972).

Run Your Own Business, P. Douglas (J. M. Dent, London, 1974).

Running Your Own Business, R. Edwards (Ward Lock, London, 1979).

Your Business – the Right Way to Run It, A. Elliot (Elliot Right Way Books, 1976).

Be Your Own Boss, A. Fiber (Management Books, London, 1975).

Working for Yourself – the Daily Telegraph Guide to Self-Employment, G. Golzen (Kogan Page, London, annually).

Managing the Survival of Smaller Companies, A. C. Hazel & A. S. Red (Business Books, London, 1978).

Your Business Problems Solved, P. Jenner (David & Charles, Newton Abbot, 1979).

How to be Your Own Boss, Hugh Kinnaird (Hutchinson, London, 1975).
It Can be Done, J. M. Ryan (Scope Books, Newbury, 1979).
Basic Business Management Guidelines for the Self-Employed and the Smaller Business, M. A. Peters (Jordans, Bristol, 1978).
Buying a Shop?: A Daily Telegraph Guide, A. St. J. Price (Kogan Page, London, 1979).
Starting and Running a Small Business, A. Sproxton (United Writers, St Ives, 1979).
Starting Your Own Business, A. Taylor (Moore, Elland; Yorkshire, 1975).
Bigger Profits for the Smaller Firm, E. G. Wood (Business Books, London, 1972).
The Guardian Guide to Running a Small Business, Clive Woodcock (Kogan Page, 1980).

See articles in the Business News section of the *Sunday Times*; also the *Financial Times*, *Guardian*, *Daily Telegraph* and *Management Today*.